"Above all, these two experience  **S0-BYN-383** and personal experience to help us through the most difficult transition—from midlife autonomy to increasing interdependence. Aimed at helpers, the book also invites us to be the ones walking the path of diminishment with dignity and grace. We all need to know this terrain!"

—Marjory Bankson, author of *Creative Aging:*
Rethinking Retirement in a Changing World

"Our elders 'have gone before us on a road . . . we too will travel.' The authors quote Socrates, and then they present a plainspoken, insightful guidebook that illuminates a road many of us regard with dread, uncertainty, and the natural desire to put off to another day. This is a practical book, both honest and nonthreatening. It is full of wisdom that family members of several generations can use together, as they seek loving and respectful compromises to the dilemmas of old age."

—Ann Barnet, MD, Founder, Family Place, Washington, DC
Coauthor (with husband Richard Barnet) of *The Youngest Minds*

"Judge Carolyn Miller Parr and Sig Cohen have authored a comprehensive guide for families preparing to care for an older adult member or planning their own future as elders. Their stories and suggestions about how to navigate the legal, emotional, and financial challenges ahead offer invaluable advice and evocative reading."

—William Fralin, JD, Elder Law Attorney
Founder, The Estate Planning and Elder Law Firm, PC
Alexandria, Virginia, and Washington, DC

"Carolyn Parr and Sig Cohen's book, particularly the chapter on siblings, gives practical and time-honored advice on the frustrating family dynamics that sometimes impact even well-adjusted families. *Love's Way: Living Peacefully with Your Family as Your Parents Age* is a great tool to add to your family emotional toolkit."

—Marti Bailey, BS, CSA, CDP
Director, Sibley Senior Association and Community Health

"Anxious about talking with a parent or an aging relative about their living arrangements? This is your book! The authors' rich background in law and mediation come together to challenge our incorrect assumptions, while providing clear and respectful ways to discuss and approach the questions around caring for aging people and their families. Members of all ages in my church participated in a highly popular study around this book, with immediately positive results as they had the courage and the tools to directly address this issue in their families. This book not only helps people think through everything about caring for their parents, but it also helps them plan ahead for themselves!"

—Rev. Ryan P. Sirmons, Pastor
The United Church of Christ of Annapolis, Maryland

"In *Love's Way*, coauthors Carolyn Parr and Sig Cohen help address the universal dysfunction of families' failure to plan by removing some of the barriers that prevent the conversations that need to take place. Breaking down the communication styles, learning and relearning family roles, understanding the past but seeing the future, and accepting changes and decline are but a few of the tools addressed in this helpful book for individuals and their families. How fortunate for all of us that the authors have chosen to share their professional techniques and experiential mediation history to help us move forward with our relationships and planning to affect optimum life outcomes."

—Maureen Cavaiola, Cofounder, Partners in Care
Founder, At Home Chesapeake and Geriatric Care
Manager, Aging Life Association

LOVE'S WAY

LIVING
PEACEFULLY
WITH YOUR FAMILY
AS
YOUR PARENTS
AGE

LOVE'S

WAY

CAROLYN MILLER PARR

&

SIG COHEN

Love's Way: Living Peacefully with Your Family as Your Parents Age

© 2019 Carolyn Miller Parr and Sig Cohen
Hendrickson Publishers Marketing, LLC
P. O. Box 3473
Peabody, Massachusetts 01961-3473
www.hendrickson.com

ISBN 978-1-68307-195-2

All Scripture quotations, unless otherwise indicated, are taken from the Holy Bible, New Revised Standard Version (NRSV), copyright © 1989, National Council of the Churches of Christ in the United States of America. Used by permission. All rights reserved.

Printed in the United States of America

First Printing—January 2019

Library of Congress Cataloging-in-Publication Data

A catalog record for this title is available from the Library of Congress
Hendrickson Publishers Marketing, LLC ISBN 978-1-68307-195-2

Contents

Preface

In their mediation practice with adult families, Carolyn Parr and Sig Cohen have discovered a crying need for this book, a need that is only growing more intense as the Baby Boomer generation ages.

The authors are themselves in the last third of life. They have each navigated the shoals of caring for their own parents at life's end. They have a strong record of accompanying "invisible" people living on the edge, as the elderly often feel. And Carolyn and Sig are professional mediators with more than forty years' experience between them.

The authors' work is the fruit of their dedication to public and community service, first with the United States Government, then with faith-based communities and underserved populations. As a Foreign Service officer in the United States Information Agency, Sig spent more than half his career overseas. Carolyn is a lawyer and retired judge. Recipients of their community service have included callers to a suicide hotline, abused and neglected children, refugees, and homeless men and women with AIDS.

Sig and Carolyn met through the District of Columbia Superior Court's mediation program and since 2002 have focused on families in distress. In the cases of older parents with adult children, the authors discovered that the pain came from two sources: broken relationships within the family, and a parent's failure to plan for the end of life. From that discovery, *Love's Way* was born.

Elders are storytellers. The stories here stem from the authors' own families, friends, and mediation clients. While names and identifying details have been changed to protect privacy, the stories contained herein are true.

Acknowledgments

We are filled with gratitude and so much love for our spouses, Susan Cohen and Jim Le Gette. Their patience and support as we wrestled with rough drafts, and their faith in us when we doubted, helped bring this book to life.

Thanks also to our outstanding agent, Karen Harding, who believed in us; Patricia Anders, our very talented editor at Hendrickson Publishers, whose encouraging comments and gentle edits made our book better; and Hendrickson's PR gurus Meg Rusick and Maggie Swofford who are teaching us how to market.

Emily Turek, our faithful social media director and assistant, kept us on schedule with social media, our blog, and newsletter, when our minds were elsewhere.

Arline Kardasis and Crystal Thorpe, our trainers from Elder Decisions, taught us the specialized ins and outs of elder mediation and started us on this journey. Gail Dudley, publisher of *Ready* magazine, and Cheryl Jamison, executive director of the Association for Conflict Resolution, offered opportunities for podcasts.

Sincerest gratitude to Kimberly Parr for her reading and advice; William Fralin, Marjorie Bankson, Ann Barnet, Ryan Sirmons, Maureen Cavaiola, and Marti Bailey for believing in us enough to endorse us. M. Jane Markley's guidance about health-care planning was invaluable.

Susan Wranik, Steve Gurney, and the staff at DC Senior Resources Group offered speaking opportunities. Thanks to Sally White and the staff at Iona Senior Center, including Deborah Rubenstein and Dixcy Bosley-Smith as well as Suzy Elder Murphy and her colleagues at Debra Levy Eldercare Associates for their advice and support. We cannot forget our marketing guru Jeanne Stanislawski who helped us get local prominence.

A special shout-out to Carolyn's writer sisters at Redbud Writers Guild for generously sharing their knowledge and support.

And finally, thanks to our clients and friends from our faith communities, who trusted us with the stories (identifying details of which have been changed to protect privacy) that make the book come alive.

Carolyn and Sig

INTRODUCTION

"I loved my dad. I wish I'd told him while he was alive." Dan's voice caught and his hands shook as he looked down from the pulpit on his father's closed casket. Father and son had not spoken to each other for a decade. Standing before the mourners, Dan found it hard to recall what exactly caused him to leave home and never look back. Until it was too late.

One imagines that if the tables had been turned—if the father were standing before Dan's casket—he'd have felt the same way. Responsibility for this broken relationship had likely been shared.

None of us wants to leave our loved ones a legacy of guilt. Whether we are fifty or eighty, we hope others will remember us with love and admiration. We hope we'll be missed. We hope the causes we care about will go on.

The secret to creating that reality is deceptively simple but hard to embody. In *How to Say it to Seniors*, David Solie suggests that only three things are required:

1. *Acceptance* of our losses, so we don't get trapped in bitterness or despair;

2. *Humility* to look honestly at where we missed the mark; and

3. *Courage* to change where change is needed.[1]

We (the writers) are colleagues in a mediation practice. We are no longer young. We've arrived at the stage where our own fifty-something kids begin to worry about our safety—and maybe wonder whether it's time for us to move. But personal safety, according

---

1. David Solie, *How to Say It to Seniors: Closing the Communications Gap with Our Elders* (New York: Prentice Hall, 2004).

to Dr. Atul Gawande is not a primary third-age concern.[2] Seniors care more about maintaining the freedom to make their own decisions, especially decisions about how they will die.

Even while clinging to our independence, however, down in the hidden chambers of our hearts, we may entertain a fleeting worry: How will we manage when we can no longer drive? Or if we fall and break a bone? Or, God forbid, we begin to lose our memories? Will our autonomy slip away as we begin to depend on others? Maybe the better question is: *How can we allow independence to soften into interdependence?*

Every day in our work we meet loving parents, adult children, and siblings who want to do the right thing but keep colliding with one another's fears and boundaries. Even so, our clients teach us that adult children and their parents can coexist in their later years with grace and generosity of spirit. Starting now, we can strengthen the bonds we share and make it easier for our children to love and care for each other when we are gone.

Though we are mediators, this book is not about mediation. It is about how seniors and their children can nurture those relationships that work and heal those that don't, how family members can listen to each other with understanding and love, and how siblings can learn to put away childhood resentments and embrace the persons their brothers and sisters have become. It's about how families can plan for the future together, in a way that respects the dignity and autonomy of parents and the emotional and practical needs of children, so that they can grow together in love, even as they embark on the difficult but necessary journey toward the end of life.

---

2. Atul Gawande, *Being Mortal: Medicine and What Matters in the End* (New York: Henry Holt, 2014).

1

Not Your Grandma's Old

*"I enjoy talking with very old people. They have gone before
us on a road by which we, too, may have to travel, and
I think we do well to learn from them what it is like."*

Socrates in Plato's *The Republic*

"I did it to make him notice me."

Geneva, an eighty-something woman, was embroiled in a protracted and ugly lawsuit with her adult son, James. Rather than rule
on the case, the judge ordered them to mediation, hoping she and her
son would avoid an emotionally debilitating and costly legal battle.

As mediator in the case, Carolyn was surprised by Geneva's
candor. Geneva explained that, without warning, she closed her
joint bank account with her only son while he and his family were
on vacation. James discovered this when he tried to pay taxes on his
and his mother's jointly owned beach house, as previously agreed.
When James called his mother to ask what was up, she snapped
"Talk to my lawyer!" and hung up.

Things swiftly careened downhill. Geneva's lawyer persuaded
her to sue James to get his name off the deed. James counterclaimed
for half the rent money, which until then both parties had regarded
solely as his mother's. Now they glared at each other across the mediation table. James was hurt and puzzled by his mother's behavior.
He had never misused their bank account and couldn't imagine
why she had closed it.

But here's the backstory. When Geneva was sick and hospitalized, she wanted James to handle her finances. When she recovered,
she began to resent her loss of control. Rent checks in both names

now came to James (who duly deposited them in their joint account). Bank statements also came to James. Then, when Geneva called the property manager to question a plumber's bill, she was told, "I deal with your son. Ask him." By closing the bank account, Geneva was making a plea—one she couldn't bring herself to voice directly: "Look at me, Son! Listen to me! I can still make decisions. I can still think. I'm not helpless. I'm not invisible!"

In the mediation session, mother and son finally listened to each other, and they agreed to leave the title in joint names and set up an escrow account for the rent money. That solved the legal problem. Although mending feelings would take longer, both wanted to reconcile. Geneva admitted she shouldn't have closed the account without talking to James. James saw that he'd been insensitive to his mother's need for autonomy. They agreed to have dinner together once a week and to share honestly whatever was on their minds—even if it required a tough conversation.

Geneva and James's story is not unique. As our parents age, they not only shrink physically but also may fade from our awareness. When they retire, rarely does anyone from their old job call to ask their advice. If they become chronically ill or lack sufficient energy to venture out, they can easily become isolated and lonely. Family and friends don't mean to abandon them; but until there's a crisis, a homebound senior often vanishes from their thoughts. Clerks ignore them. Servers ask their companion what the senior wants to eat. Their footprint on the world becomes smaller, and they can feel as if they're disappearing.

"I'm Not Your Grandma's Old"

I was having coffee with my friend Sadia when our conversation turned to aging and how to address changes in our children's perceptions about older people. Sadia told me that when her son recently became "overly concerned" about her well-being, she replied, "I'm not your Grandma's old."

"Your grandmother's *old*?" I wondered. What on earth did she mean? Sadia explained that in the twenty-first century, our lives are different from how our parents' were when they were our age. Most of us are healthier, consume a better diet, smoke less, and keep up with current events. Many of us work at least part time after retiring from our first job. We may decide to start a new business, take up writing or art, or become involved with a nonprofit organization. Subjected as we are to information that is ubiquitous because of the Internet, we can't help but stay abreast of new medical advances and how to minimize if not avoid chronic illnesses. As a result, we live longer.

Sadia noted that most of us are better able to cope with stress, our minds are more alive, and we look for new ways to stay engaged in our community. The lifestyles and well-being of today's seniors mean that they are more active and able to live independently longer than our parents when they were in their seventies and eighties.

Indeed, as children grow up and their parents age, family dynamics are bound to change. But not always for the better. When younger people think of their parents, many are stuck with the image of their grandparents—but that may not be where your own parents are today.

Geezer or Honored Citizen?

In 2017, my wife and I traveled to Portland, Oregon. We had a wonderful visit. There was so much to see, the weather was awesome, and our hotel was top notch. On our first evening there, we took in a play at the Artists' Repertory Theater. The theater houses several arts organizations, including "The Geezer Gallery." When I saw that name, I did a double take.

After years of writing about ageism and the need for older Americans to face life with self-respect and dignity, I was taken aback. When older adults have so many perception hurdles already to navigate, why create yet another one? True, the mission of "The Geezer Gallery" is to showcase talented senior artists and create art therapy programs aimed at the Portland's senior community. But "Geezer"? Although I subsequently learned that many Portlanders like the name "Geezer Gallery," I personally find it self-deprecating.

While in Portland, we used the trolley system. When we bought our tickets, one price option was for "Honored Citizens." Not *Senior*

Citizens. We knew Portland prides itself on being "weird," but what a contrast: An art venue for seniors called "The Geezer Gallery" and a trolley system that refers to seniors as "Honored Citizens."

For us, the contrast is another example of how many younger persons perceive older adults. They're viewed as odd, weak, even cranky. While at other times, they are seen as experienced, more patient, and even wise.

Barriers to Communication

The Perception Gap

Although an increasing proportion of the world's population is aging, a popular attitude toward aging (at least in the United States) does not follow Socrates' view of enjoying "talking with very old people" and how "we would do well to learn from them." Many see it as a period of weakness, infirmity, and diminished capacity.

In his 2014 book *Second Wind,* geriatrician Dr. Bill Thomas wrote:

> The psychological and emotional terrain of elder-hood is poorly understood by young and old alike. In place of wisdom and insight, our culture has presented us with superficial and misleading explanations for why elders behave the way they do. This lack of understanding is, for example, largely responsible for the well-known archetype of the "grumpy old man."[1]

Dr. Thomas is not alone. In a 2015 report, the Frameworks Institute observed:

> The public's dominant *real* models of aging includes shared understandings of aging as a process of deterioration, dependency, reduced potential, family dispersal, and digital incompetence. These deep and negative shared understandings make the process of aging something to be dreaded and fought against, rather than embraced as a process that brings new opportunities and challenges for individuals and society.[2]

---

1. Bill Thomas, *Second Wind* (New York: Simon & Schuster, 2014), 208.
2. Eric Lindland, Marissa Fond, Abigail Haydon, and Nathaniel Kendall-Taylor, "Gauging Aging: Mapping the Gaps between Expert and Public Under-

Role Reversal

When we were growing up, Mom and Dad were the permission givers, advisors, financiers, shelter providers, big-picture framers, and decision-makers. Now children want to advise parents about the parents' safety, finances, and care. As a result, parents may feel anything from relief to resentment.

In her song "God is in the Roses," Roseanne Cash describes sitting at the grave of her father, Johnny Cash, and writing, "I love you like a brother, a father, and a son." These words describe the changing roles we all play in relationships as we and those we love age. We begin as our parent's child. Then we may move into an egalitarian role, more like our parent's friend or advisor in an area of our own expertise.

For example, I turn to my kids when my computer hiccups, and they turn to me with their tax questions. We are partners, or more like siblings. But imperceptibly, as the parent relies on the adult child more and more, the child gradually becomes more responsible, indispensable, and more like a parent. This can be challenging for everyone. Indeed, it becomes another layer of loss for both generations.

As our roles change, our emotional landscape may also change. If a parent (or spouse or friend) is in the early stages of memory loss, then we may become cross and impatient. We think they are not listening, not paying attention. We may experience denial, because the possibility of early stage dementia can be too painful. We may sound irritated when we're really frustrated or exasperated. We lecture them. We may even blame them for something they did unwittingly. The parent may also become angry and frustrated. This changing family dynamic is painful, challenging—and scary.

Caregiving children must be especially wary. Once we begin caring for others, especially our parents, we feel responsible. We want to do the right thing, but we often come up against a different way of thinking and doing. While a younger person may prefer to pursue matters linearly, an older adult may want to take a more roundabout (and time-consuming) approach.

standing of Aging in America," *A Frameworks Strategic Report*, Frameworks Institute, 6 (New York: Simon & Schuster, 2015). Used by permission.

New communication skills may be required. It can be helpful to listen twice as much as you speak. When a person feels genuinely heard, it feels like love. The cost is little, but the value great. Listening is not the same as agreeing. It brings a double blessing: healing to the speaker and deeper understanding to the listener.

Ignorance

Ignorance is the third barrier to understanding our aging parents. Though most seniors remain fit and active for many years, they will eventually encounter medical problems. Most of us have no idea what it's like to use a walker, drag around an oxygen tank, wear adult diapers, or cope with a failing memory. No matter how sympathetic we may feel, it's unlikely we'll understand the sadness, humiliation, resignation, and forbearance many elders experience as their horizons narrow and their options diminish. And it's so easy to rush to judgment about their reduced capacity.

If we reflect on our parents' losses and diminishments with an open heart, then our outlook will shift. Imagine, even briefly, how frightening it must be to lose your independence, how depressing (and boring) to spend your days in a wheelchair watching TV soaps, perhaps in a drug-induced stupor designed to keep you "under control."

Rushing to judgment is like driving a speeding car. You focus on the road ahead, not the world around you. Walking in another's shoes can engender greater generosity of spirit, going the extra mile, ceding the benefit of the doubt, or listening with an open heart. Saying "I will defer judgment and look at the situation from your point of view" means entering a shared world—if only for a brief time—with your aging parent, disabled brother, or disoriented loved one.

Autonomy versus Safety

In our mediation practice, we often see conflicts arise between aging parents and their children around autonomy versus safety. As Dr. Atul Gawande notes, "Safety is what we want for those we love. Autonomy is what we want for ourselves."[3]

---

3. Atul Gawande, *Being Mortal: Medicine and What Matters in the End* (New York: Henry Holt, 2014), 106.

Intergenerational conflicts arise when families need to decide whether elderly parents should stop driving, where and with whom they should live, and what kinds of medical treatment they should receive. These decisions become more crucial as a parent nears the end of life. Often parents prefer autonomy to safety, while their adult children opt for the opposite. As mediators, we ask ourselves: How can we help these adult families find solutions that recognize the value of both?

In the 2008 film *Gran Torino*, Clint Eastwood plays Walt Kowalski, a curmudgeonly Korean War veteran who literally throws his older son out of his home when the son suggests Walt move into a retirement community. For the son, the overriding issue may have been his dad's safety. (Or it may have been getting money and control of the family home.) Kowalski's sole concern was independence.

Ask your parent: "What's most important for you?" If a parent is worried about leaving behind his beloved dog Jack when moving into an independent living community, then any provision for Dad's move should include Jack. If Aunt Millie's goal is to finish knitting an afghan for her new granddaughter before undergoing a major medical procedure, then lower doses of a mind-numbing pain medication may be advised rather than the full prescription so she can remain mentally alert. If an elder's faith community is his primary source of spiritual support and social activity, then he will want to reside near his congregation and have easily accessible transportation to it. If Mom wants to age in her own home, then whatever arrangements are made for her care should give precedence to aging there over other concerns.

Talking in an Inexorably Shrinking World

While adults in their seventies ordinarily can manage very well, what's left for older adults in their eighties, nineties, and beyond? One major health event can propel them from "young old age" to "old old age." At that point, loss of autonomy is all around. Friends have died. They can't drive at night, or maybe not at all. Mobility may be hampered by hip replacement surgery, a history of falling, dementia, or other physical and psychological impairments. Other factors include loneliness and isolation or a changing (demographically, racially, economically) neighborhood. Unfamiliarity with technological changes can also overwhelm them.

As we have seen, many older adults feel they must clutch onto whatever remnants of their independence remain intact. No wonder the aging process is so frightening, both to older parents and the children who love them. What can we do to ease an older adult's entry into "old old age"?

1. Listen to comprehend, not to argue.

2. Try to build confidence, not anxiety.

3. Understand that these conversations are a process, not a one-shot event. They may take multiple sessions over days, if not weeks.

4. Focus on the issue, not the individual. If you're concerned about your parents' safety, focus on that and not their attitude, perceived intractability, or resistance.

5. If the conversation becomes too emotional, stop. Take a break. Change the subject. Don't let the discussion get out of hand.

6. Make sure you understand what you want to discuss. If it's about moving to an assisted living residence, have you checked out its location, cost, amenities, and so on? If it's about Mom no longer driving, do you know your state's laws regarding driver's licenses for older adults? Available public transportation?

7. As long as they remain competent, respect your parents' right to control their own destiny, even if you disagree with their decision.

While conversations between adult kids and their parents are crucial, they may be inhibited by fear. Keep listening. It's the most powerful resource we have to breach the walls of resistance and silence. Together, families can create a new story—one guided by love and understanding. The path toward a happy ending begins with trying to walk together, even for a short time, in another's shoes.

2

Transforming Fear and Anger

by Carolyn

"Don't move the way fear makes you move."

Rumi

Creating a Legacy of Hope Together Requires Courage

Do your parents have a will? Do you? Writing a will is intimidating, at any age. It brings us face to face with our mortality. It also forces us to think about money—how we've spent it, how to divide it, how it might be used for good. And it reminds us of the reality that we can't take it with us.

Fear can paralyze. A parent may be thinking, *Giving someone else the right to sign my name (a power of attorney [POA]) feels like a frightening loss of control, even if I lock it up and just tell the holder where to find it when it's needed.* Similarly, giving another the power to make one's health care decisions if incapacitated and creating an advance directive (a living will) whisper: *There's likely to be suffering at your life's end.*

And as for those relationships that need mending, in and out of the family: *Shouldn't I just let sleeping dogs lie?*

Scary stuff.

Whether you're the child or the parent, taking action on any of these issues—distributing assets, health care, improving relationships—must begin with a conversation. Some of these conversations may be challenging. But . . .

Doing Nothing Is Worse

Who should initiate the conversation? It's probably easier if the parent does, but either generation can start. If you think talking about end-of-life matters raises anxiety, avoiding the conversation is even worse.

It's not unusual for adult siblings to go to war with one another when parents leave no testamentary plan or have failed to update the one they had. One elder wanted to provide for her grandchildren's education. She named those who had been born when the will was written but she didn't update her plan to include those grandchildren who were born later. Then a stroke rendered her incapacitated. She left her eight children alienated from one another, perhaps forever. While some of their older children were able to go to college, there was no provision for the younger ones to do so.[1]

If parents fail to act, then others—their relatives, the state, or a court—will act for them in ways they may not have foreseen or desired. The good news is that when family members summon up the courage to begin the conversation, together they can discover and create the larger meaning of their sojourn together on the face of the earth.

Naming the Fears

The first and toughest conversation will be with yourself. What are you afraid of? Here are some of the fears our clients have named about entering a tough conversation:

- Fear of making the situation worse
- Fear of hurting the other's feelings
- Fear of alienating the other
- Fear of being wrong

---

1. Watch the "Black Heirlooms" video and be inspired by the surprising bittersweet ending of this true cautionary tale as the grandchildren (cousins) jointly decide to come together in spite of their parents' enduring hostility toward each other. See https://www.youtube.com/watch?v=Y9olFkZ18J4.

- Fear of having to change

- Fear of your own or the other's anger

The first hurdle to conquer is fear itself.

"Just 25 Percent?"

"How would your life change if you could reduce your fear level by just 25 percent?" Pastor Gordon Cosby challenged me with this question years ago.

I was a United States Tax Court Judge at that time and leery of doing anything that might look controversial. For instance, I was afraid to participate in peaceful demonstrations for causes I believed in, even matters that could never possibly come before my court. I wanted to volunteer in an AIDS hospice, but I was afraid my colleagues might ostracize me. I wrote songs but was afraid to sing them to others for fear of losing my dignity. Though others thought I was powerful, I was a mess of unacknowledged fears.

I did eventually march and sing and become braver in many places in my life. But from time to time, I still struggle with Gordon's question. And there's always that pesky fear of failing.

Naming your fear is a first step. But how do you shrink it down to manageable size?

Shrinking the Fear

When Eleanor Roosevelt married her cousin, Franklin Delano Roosevelt, she was painfully shy and gripped by low self-esteem. Her mother-in-law ridiculed Eleanor's hair. Comedians imitated her grating voice. Cartoonists emphasized her disappearing chin. Her unfashionable clothes draped a shapeless body.

Yet Eleanor's compassion drove her to become the voice of the voiceless. In the process, she became one of the world's most respected women in the twentieth century.

How did she do it? She told the world her secret: "Do one thing every day that scares you." Here's how to work with that.

Do What Scares You in Stages

Start with small steps. The first time I participated in a demonstration, I wore a scarf that partially hid my face and I avoided cameras. I did not carry a sign or offer to speak. I stayed in the middle of the marchers. I wanted my presence to swell the crowd, but I did not want to be noticed or identified. I felt very brave when the march was over. I had survived!

I didn't cover my face the next time.

Maybe you're afraid of a difficult conversation you need to have with a family member or work colleague. You might start with a request: "Could we have lunch one day next week? I'd like to share some thoughts with you and get your views."

Let's say you want to approach your sister about sharing the cost of a helper for Mom, but you're afraid she'll resist or become defensive or angry. Start the lunchtime conversation by describing your concern in nonjudgmental language, and then ask how your sister sees it. For instance, you might say, "When I visited Mom last week I noticed dirty dishes all over the kitchen and very little food in the fridge. I'm worried. What do you think might be going on?"

Then you listen. Follow where the conversation leads. During that first lunch you may or may not get around to the topic of cost sharing, but you can offer to gather information and meet again. These are small steps that will make you less fearful of the next conversation, increase your knowledge about what's happening with Mom, and explore your sister's willingness to help deal with it.

Do What Scares You with a Companion

Eons of human experience show that we are braver when we are not alone. There was a reason Jesus sent out his disciples two by two. It's one reason why people get married. We can take greater risks because we know someone has our back. There's less chance of making an error if I have a companion with whom I can talk it over. If one of us is scared, the other may be brave. We can share our knowledge and experience. We inspire each other.

Having a companion also creates accountability. When we commit to try something new, we are more likely to follow through if another is expecting it. Jesus may have gotten the idea from Ecclesiastes 4:9–12 in the Hebrew Bible:

> Two are better than one, because they have a good reward for their toil. For if they fall, one will lift up the other; but woe to one who is alone and falls and does not have another to help. Again, if two lie together, they keep warm; but how can one keep warm alone? And though one might prevail against another, two will withstand one.

Do What Scares You with a Mediator

A major benefit of mediation is the simple presence of another person. With a neutral third party in the room, participants feel safer to express what they want and need. And when people feel less afraid, they are less defensive and more willing to negotiate, freer to apologize, to make requests, and to bring up sensitive topics.

Experienced mediators don't just sit there. They'll reframe, summarize, ask open questions, and use other techniques that create a safe space for dialogue and therefore greatly reduce the danger of participants permanently hurting or alienating one another. Mediators will focus on finding areas of common ground and creating a useful process for the parties to employ should future disputes arise. They'll provide opportunities for separate, confidential conversations with the mediator if sensitive topics need to be addressed privately. They'll teach the parties how to listen to understand (rather than refute) and how to speak so as to be heard. They'll help the parties brainstorm solutions that work for everyone. Some of those techniques are described more extensively in chapter 3.

What If I Try and Fail?

To keep going in spite of fear, sometimes we just need to *lower our expectations*. During World War II, Etty Hillesum, a young Jewish woman from Holland, had a chance to escape the Nazi occupiers. But she chose to go to the death camps with her people. She wrote in her journal: "As life becomes harder and more threatening, it also becomes richer, because the fewer expectations we have, the more the good things of life become unexpected gifts which we accept with gratitude."[2]

In *Bird by Bird*, her book about writing, Anne Lamott talks about the paralysis of perfectionism.[3] She says that when she has writer's block she types "[Trashy] First Draft" at the top of a blank page. I tried that and was amazed at how quickly the fear of making a mistake disappeared with a giggle.

Lamott also contends that it's healthy to make lots of mistakes. As my colleague Joel Gerber once said about his damaged runner's knees, "I think of them as battle scars." The trick is managing to get up and start again when we fall down.

We often avoid starting a tough conversation because we're afraid "it won't work." Here's one way to overcome that concern: Redefine "success." Success doesn't have to mean the other person accepts your proposed solution. It may mean something as simple as learning what the other person really needs (that is, you are listening to understand) and expressing your own needs in a compassionate way. Then you search together for common ground.

It may be as simple as reframing the issue to include everyone's interests.

When my parents were in their late eighties, they came to live with my husband Jerry and me. Mom had Alzheimer's and did not recognize me. Dad was her caregiver. It was a muggy summer in Washington, DC, with temperatures in the 90s. Mom immediately complained about the air conditioning at night and kept trying to adjust the first-floor thermostat from 77 degrees to off. We'd discover this only when our second-floor bedroom became unbearable. We needed to talk.

I thought the issue was "How do we get Mom to stop messing with the thermostat?" We went downstairs to talk with them. They were wearing sweaters. And I realized it was ten degrees cooler there than the first floor, and even cooler still than our bedroom.

---

2. Etty Hillesum, *An Interrupted Life, The Diaries 1941–1943* (New York: Picador, 1996).

3. Anne Lamott, *Bird by Bird: Some Instructions on Writing and Life* (New York: Anchor, 1995).

It really *was* too cold for frail old people. So the issue changed to "How can we make the temperature at night bearable for all of us?"

Jerry and I immediately figured out the solution when, walking our shih-tzu pups in a nearby alley the next day, we spied a perfectly good window air conditioner with a give-away sign. Jerry installed it in our bedroom window, we turned off the central air at night, and everybody slept well the rest of the summer.

Fear of Anger

"I can't talk to her because she'll get mad." Or, "I'm afraid I'll lose my temper." Ever been stuck in a churning loop of angry thought? A never-ending tape replays in your mind, reminding you of what the other person said, how it wounded you, how you wish you'd responded, how justified you were, how unfair/wrong/deceptive (you choose) the other is? Oh yeah . . . and maybe just a teeny bit of fantasizing about delicious revenge?

I have. And I don't like what anger does. It steals my sleep, distracts me when I need to concentrate, and generally makes me miserable. I feel stuck. This is what Eckhart Tolle describes when he says, "Our problem is we think too much." He says the solution is to train oneself to be "in the present moment." But how?

Jill Bolte Taylor, a Harvard-trained neurologist, was only thirty-eight years old when she suffered a massive stroke that for a while obliterated the left globe of her brain. Even though she realized what was happening as she lost the power of speech and linear thought, she felt tranquil and embraced by love.

In *My Stroke of Insight*, Dr. Taylor describes how cognitive loops from her left brain used to take her prisoner. She discovered how to "step to the right" hemisphere where inner peace, compassion, and a feeling of deep connection with all life (and mystical and religious experience) seem to reside. After her stroke, she learned she could consciously move from one hemisphere to the other (which also reduces fear).[4]

---

4. Jill Bolte Taylor, *My Stroke of Insight: A Brain Scientist's Personal Journey* (New York: Penguin, 2008).

Here are some of her practical tips to "step to the right": Breathe deeply. Watch your belly inflate. Hold the breath. Exhale. Do it again. Move: Stretch, exercise, dance, do yoga or Tai chi. Run up and down the stairs. (When we're focusing on our bodies, we're not stuck in our minds.) Sing—listen to music that soothes your spirit. Get lost in the arts.

Rilke's poetry does it for me. Sig rides his bike long distances. You might wander in an art gallery. Walk in the rain, feel the breeze, climb a hill, and throw your arms wide to the sky. Pray, meditate, worship, say a mantra. Use your senses: take a hot bath, get a massage, taste something new and wonderful. Hug someone you love.

Dr. Taylor also recommends a deliberate focus on appreciation and gratitude for life. For years I've kept a "gratitude journal." I try every day to give thanks for what is. I consciously affirm the "not yet" by envisioning what I long for and sending positive energy into the universe (I call it prayer).

Anger: A Screen for Fear

Anger may feel primary, but in reality it's a secondary emotion. For instance, it can be a screen for fear. When somebody has really ticked me off, it helps to ask myself, "What am I afraid of?" It may be simply losing face (if the other person has been disrespectful). But it could involve a more serious loss or some kind of injustice that needs to be directly addressed. The anger is not the problem. It is the fear beneath the anger that is crying out to be named.

Anger can also be a mask for pain. In her seminal work, *On Death and Dying*, Dr. Elizabeth Kubler Ross named anger as one of the five stages of grief. (The others are denial, bargaining, depression, and acceptance.) Your parents may be stuck in anger because they are grieving life-changing losses: career, health, mobility, independence, or the death of a spouse.

When we peer behind each of our angers, we see words unspoken, pain postponed, and disappointments unreconciled. Anger isn't always bad; it can also be a source of energy. It can ease the end of a bad love affair or the loss of a job you relished. It can help you fight for justice. But don't get stuck there. A support group, especially for elders going through the losses imposed by aging, can be a big help. Sharing the load with others in your situation may empower you to traverse anger and move on to the calm waters of healing.

Ten Tips to Defuse Anger

This all sounds pretty theoretical. But what can you do in the moment when conversation gets loud and aggressive and tempers flare? Here are some practical tips:

1. Breathe. Ask for a time-out if you need it.

2. Make a request. "Could you please lower your voice?"

3. Listen without interrupting, if possible. Listen to understand where the other is coming from, not to refute.

4. Repeat as accurately as possible what you heard the person saying, so they will know they've been heard. Then ask, "Have I understood you? Is there anything else?"

5. Ask for clarification (for instance, of possible assumptions or ambiguous terms). "Can you give me an example of what I did when you thought I was being disrespectful?"

6. Ask, "What is most frustrating/painful/upsetting about this for you?"

7. If they go on and on, it's okay to interrupt and ask, "Can you tell me what you need?"

8. Name the points of their argument that you agree with or concede.

9. Acknowledge any new information you learned from what they said.

10. Give an affirmation: "Now I understand why you are upset." Note: You're not agreeing with their perspective, but you're not arguing with it either. If their anger is based on an inaccurate assumption—such as misreading your intention or missing information—then yes, you do understand why they're upset. Pause to take it all in and then ask, "Now may I tell you how I see it?"

Chances are, the anger will dissipate and the other will, in fact, be ready to listen. Then you get on with seeking a solution—together.

Making testamentary plans, creating powers of attorney, writing an advance directive, repairing relationships, engaging in tough conversations, and defusing anger all have something in common besides the fear they induce: *At bottom, they're all expressions of love.* Move the way love leads, and the fear will dissipate.

That's because the opposite of fear may not be courage. Perhaps the opposite of fear is love. And it is love that will give you the strength and the will to engage in a tough conversation with mutual respect and patience.

3

CAN WE JUST TALK?

BY SIG

Roy and Elizabeth's Story

As eighty-year-old Elizabeth let herself into the apartment, she sensed something was wrong. "Roy?" she called. Then, fighting panic, "Roy? Roy!"

"Over here." Roy was on the dining room floor, where he'd fallen six hours earlier.

Roy, eighty-four, was fully conscious but had been unable to get up or to call for help. He walked haltingly with a walker, and his legs hurt unbearably much of the time. At the hospital, doctors suspected he'd suffered a small stroke. After a couple of days, they sent him home.

Elizabeth and Roy have a son three hours away and a daughter six hours. Both kids love their parents. They came immediately and said, "We want you to move in with us. Or at least near us. We'll find you a place you'll like."

Roy said, "We're fine. We're staying here." The kids felt desperate. It's obvious their parents were not fine. They didn't know whether their parents had wills or insurance, or where they stored their important papers. Roy and Elizabeth refused to discuss the obvious elephant in the family living room: their growing weakness and a totally foreseeable crisis about to strike.

The kids suspected the sticking point was Elizabeth's job. She still worked full time as a telephone customer service rep. She loved her job, and she was good at it. It provided status, social life, and money. It gave her life meaning. If they moved away, she knew that at her age she'd never work again.

The parents refused to have "The Conversation."

Resistance

We recently learned from an AARP publication that people's responses to the need for a tough conversation usually fall into one of three categories: resistance, reluctance, or readiness. This applies to both older adults and adult children. Roy and Elizabeth (and *Gran Torino*'s Walt Kowalski) have something in common. They embody resistance.

Fear plays a big role here. Many older adults resist engaging in "The Conversation" about their wills, plans, and wishes as they age because they fear losing their independence and the freedom to change their minds. Adult children hesitate to push the issue because they're afraid they'll upset their parents or seem greedy. And both parents and children hate to think about their parents' death.

Some years ago, Home Instead Senior Care surveyed one thousand American adult children in a caretaking role to learn what barriers inhibited their engaging in a necessary conversation with their parents. The most challenging hurdles to communication were:

- They were stuck in the old parent-child roles (31 percent) (see chapter 1).

- Their parents refused to engage (16 percent).

- The children weren't prepared (10 percent).

- Distance (8 percent). A phone conversation seemed too impersonal.

- Fear (5 percent).

- If it's challenging for adult children, then what could be going through the parents' minds? Defensiveness? Avoidance? Resentment? Fear? The parade of horribles that happens when a parent or spouse has no plan is described in chapter 6. Making the plan (a will, power of attorney, final wishes) is absolutely crucial. Whether (and how much) parents want to tell their children about their plan is a related but separate question.

Parents may be willing to talk about some things (such as whether they have a will or the name of their lawyer) but not about others (such as who gets what). Or they may reveal who will be the personal representative (executor) or trustee and who holds the power of attorney for health care, but not who has the power for financial matters. They may simply say where the documents can be found if needed.

Much depends on the family dynamics between parents and children and among siblings. More on that in chapter 5.

Before You Start "The Conversation"

We see a lot of articles about the need for family members to have "The Conversation," but not much about *how* to have it. Topics for such a talk might include what to do if an older adult falls and breaks a hip or develops a debilitating illness that requires round-the-clock care, a move to a different or safer) residence, and an advance care plan. You've already arrived at the "Moment of Change."

To the adult child: Is there anything you can do *before the conversation* to ease her fear and mitigate this life-changing event?

Yes. You can prepare yourself by doing some basic research. If Mom wants to stay in her home, how can you make that possible? *Before a crisis arises*, check on local availability and cost of home health care, as well as assisted living and nursing homes in the area. Does Mom have long-term care insurance?

What, if anything, will Medicare cover? How will Mom pay for what she needs? Who, if anyone, has her health-care power of attorney? Her financial power? (See chapter 6 for more on this.) Does Mom have a will? An advance care plan? Do you know where it is? Does her doctor have a copy? Does the local hospital? Do you?

If you live at a distance, consider engaging a local aging life care manager (sometimes called a geriatric care manager), who is a social worker specializing in elderly clients. This person will visit, interview, and then write a report of their findings and make recommendations.

To Dad or Mom: *Please be transparent.* Tell all your children your doctors' names and contact information and keep them in the loop on your prognosis. They don't need to be spared that information—they need to be able to collaborate with you for your safety, happiness, and overall well-being. Hiding information will only cause more pain in the long run.

Planning for "The Conversation" is challenging, but it's far better than sailing into uncharted territory unprepared.

How to Start

What can adult kids do to get a conversation started? One way is to start in reverse: ask your parents for advice on your own finances or wills. "Jim and I are trying to figure out how much life insurance we need and what's a good company. Do you and Mom have any? How did you decide?" Or tell them how to access your own bank accounts in case of an emergency. If they don't volunteer, then ask how to access theirs.

Then there's the scrapbook approach: That is, pull out a collection of family photos and ask a parent about a certain relative. "Where did Uncle Phil live after his wife died?" "Did your grandparents live with you when you were growing up?" "What was it like visiting Aunt Mary when she lived in a nursing home?"

You might key off something in the news, an article you read, a story you heard. Then pause and say, "Have you thought about that, Mom?"

Some conversations, in the name of human decency, simply cannot take place. For example, what can you possibly say to a mentally handicapped brother-in-law whose movements—through no fault of his own—are glacial (painfully slow) or who fails to take his meds on schedule? Or to a parent whose medical expenses are through the roof and whose resources are limited, if they even exist? Or to a spouse with dementia who keeps asking the same question over and over and over? Instead, perhaps all you can do is breathe or find a private place—to weep or scream.

Moving from Resistant to Ready: Start with Structure

If you are stonewalled on the first or second try at a serious conversation, don't be discouraged. Look for opportunities to reengage, however difficult. Be patient and tread carefully, understanding that it may take several tries before your efforts yield results.

Wading into the deep end of a tough conversation without adequate preparation can be perilous. Step carefully into the shallow end before getting in over your head—or even up to your waist!

One way to wade in is to begin with structure. Substance will come later. If, for example, I know there are important differences between the other party and me, going head to head on the issues at the start may only broaden the distance between us. So, what's the objective? I don't mean who wins and who loses. I mean, how can we frame our discussion so that we at least agree on what the outcome will look like? ("Let's try to figure out a way forward that keeps Mom safe, that she can afford, and that leaves us less stressed.")

Create a timetable: Are we in a hurry to reach a decision or do we have time? It may help move things along if we agree on a time frame. ("We'll gather information and meet again in two weeks.") Do either of us have some principles we want the other to know about? "I'm not going to consider nursing homes." Let's put bottom lines on the table before delving into substance. On the other hand, new information may change your bottom line, so try to stay as open as possible.

Nailing down structure can be a valuable step in the process. By first agreeing on these "nonissues," we will know whether we have the capacity to move forward constructively on the substance. But don't expect to open and complete the conversation in one session. Be prepared for a protracted exchange. Which can be a good thing.

Now you're ready to begin.

Listening to Understand

Basic to successfully engaging in a tough conversation is listening. Genuine listening—listening with an open heart, listening to understand—is a gift. Often, before I can complete two sentences, the other person jumps in with unsought advice or compares what I'm saying with their situation. Clearly, the other party wasn't really listening in the first place; rather, they were waiting for the right moment to pounce, to get their two cents in.

Good conversations are similar to volleying a tennis ball. Equally balanced players lob a ball back and forth over the net, intent on keeping the volley going as long as possible, not trying to score a point off the other player. Here is an example of a conversational volley that went nowhere.

Jean serves. "I'm terribly worried about my dad. Ever since his hip replacement, he hasn't been the same—"

Phyllis slams back. "Let me tell you about *my* mom. After her hip replacement, she had to move to an assisted living community . . ."

That conversational one-upmanship is like a gentle tennis serve that's returned forcefully by the other player, who is intent only on scoring her points and winning the game. (To continue the tennis analogy, she doesn't want to stay at "love all"!) But consider this gentler way to play:

Jean: "I'm terribly concerned about my dad. Ever since his hip replacement, he hasn't been the same."

Phyllis: "What seems to be the problem?"

Jean: "He appears depressed. And the stairs in his home present a real problem."

Phyllis: "That must really worry you."

Jean: "I've lost a fair amount of sleep over it."

Phyllis: "What do you think can be done to improve the situation?"

Jean: "I tried talking with him about moving to someplace where he can get some help."

Phyllis: "Any luck?"

Jean: "Nothing yet, but I want to visit Happy Acres and talk to the people there. Has this ever happened to someone in your family?"

Phyllis: "As a matter of fact, yes. My Aunt Sally had her hip replaced three or four months ago, but the occupational therapist really helped her regain her old self. Would you like her name?"

Jean: "Thank you, yes. That must be an immense relief for you and your family. How's your Aunt Sally doing?"

Phyllis: "She's still a bit ornery, but she's moving well, although a little slower."

In this match, Phyllis sincerely listened to her friend. And at some point, Jean shifted the discussion to Phyllis and her Aunt Sally. Phyllis had her own story, but she waited to tell it until asked. She also had a suggestion for a solution, but she didn't rush to "fix" Jean's problem. This was a healthy give and take.

Empathy and Compassion

Here's what else makes a conversation work: empathy and compassion. On August 20, 2013, an armed, deranged man dressed in black—Michael Brandon Hill—walked into a private school in Decatur, Georgia, intent on killing as many of the eight hundred students as he could.

Antoinette Tuff, the school's bookkeeper, was the first person Hill encountered. Armed with a loaded automatic weapon and five hundred rounds of ammunition he stormed into her office and took her hostage. Despite being terrified, she had the presence of mind to engage him in a calm and compassionate conversation. After some hours, she persuaded him to put down his weapon and surrender to the police. Miraculously, no one was injured.

What can we learn from Ms. Tuff's heroism under such extreme circumstances?

Empathy. More than anything, she expressed *empathy*. After the gunman claimed he had nothing to live for, Ms. Tuff shared with him some of her personal hardships: after thirty-three years of marriage, her husband had walked out on her, after which she'd been tempted to take her own life. She understood how he felt.

Calm. Facing a mentally ill person bent on killing, Ms. Tuff remained remarkably *calm*. She could have reacted angrily or fearfully. Instead, she had the presence of mind to treat him like anyone else who might have entered her office: with respect (calling him "sir" and later, affectionately, "baby").

Compassion. Ms. Tuff also demonstrated genuine *compassion* for Mr. Hill. She assured him, "We're not going to hurt you." She offered to serve as a human shield and walk outside the school with him so police wouldn't shoot. She even told him that she loved him and was proud of him as he relinquished his weapon and prepared to surrender to the police.

Two other elements stand out here: In addition to Ms. Tuff's calming presence of mind and abiding compassion, she didn't think Hill was a bad person, and she patiently listened to him. Someone once said, "There's nobody you couldn't like if you knew their story." She really liked him.

Ms. Tuff's empathy and compassion averted what might have been another tragic school shooting. How can we apply these qualities in our day-to-day noncrisis encounters with others?

Stay Engaged

In two long phone conversations, I found myself (intentionally) hardly uttering a word while the other parties thoroughly aired their feelings and issues. During the calls, I didn't send any text messages, sort through my e-mail, read, or do anything but listen. One caller was a brand-new acquaintance, and I hadn't talked with the other in more than two years. Yet each spoke from their hearts about their concerns.

Try this: The next time you find yourself in an extended conversation, focus your total attention on the other. Forget comparing what you heard with something you experienced. Don't try to fix the other person's situation. Don't blurt out some meaningless statement such as "I'm sure things will work out" or bring yourself into the conversation with "The same thing happened to me."

Stay on the speaker's wavelength. Let them know you hear them by reflecting what they said in language so neutral that they'll agree with you. "So let me be sure I understand how you see this . . ." Then check: "Did I get it right?" (They may modify or explain their view when they hear it back.) Ask, "Is there anything else?" If there isn't, then they're ready to hear your thoughts. Acknowledge where you agree with them and thank them for clarifying the issue. Then say, "May I tell you how I see the matter?"

Be conscious of the other person's tone and body language, as well as your own. According to *Psychology Today*, in some situations 55 percent of communication is body language, 38 percent is tone. Only 7 percent is words. Show you're listening with eye contact, leaning forward attentively, arms open or relaxed. Be aware if someone's tone and body language don't match the words you're hearing. In that case, give less weight to the words.[1]

See what happens. Notice how you feel. Did a deeper connection with the other person emerge? Did the other calm down? Notice how you lowered the temperature and narrowed the gap between you, just by the gift of listening.

Mediator Kenneth Feinberg oversaw distribution of claims arising out of the 9/11 disaster, the Virginia Tech shooting, and the BP oil spill off the Louisiana coast. He found himself listening for hours to the family members of persons killed or injured in these tragedies. In his book *Who Gets What*, Feinberg stresses the importance of allowing claimants to talk candidly about their losses. He notes that often a claimant's desire to speak about the victim—especially a loved one—was more important than the money claimed.[2]

Venting

Mediators are expected to listen to parties vent their concerns, fears, and expectations. Venting can be a normal, cathartic, and usually positive step in the process of arriving at a mediated

---

1. See https://www.psychologytoday.com/blog/beyond-words/201109/is-nonverbal-communication-numbers-game.

2. Kenneth Feinberg, *Who Gets What: Fair Compensation after Tragedy and Financial Upheaval* (New York: Public Affairs, 2012).

agreement. Some parties need to blow off steam before they'll engage in the serious work of settling a dispute. But if it goes on too long, it can add fuel to the anger and solidify positions on both sides of the table. The challenge is to listen nonjudgmentally, respectfully, and caringly.

But what if venting gets personal? Similarly to dealing with anger (see chapter 2), here are some ways to mitigate the hurt you may experience if you're the target of a vent:

- Remember, listening is not agreeing. It can be the first step in healing an emotional crisis.

- Try holding your fire until the other person finishes.

- Keep track of what was said so you can respond—but without getting emotional yourself.

- If the vent goes on interminably, ask at some point, "What do you need?" This can force the other person to state their concerns in a more orderly way.

Bear in mind that whether the dispute concerns you directly or indirectly, allowing the other party to be heard does wonders for healing someone on the other side of an issue. The person on the receiving end of a vent—whether a mediator, adversary, or loved one—needs to hold fire until the other party decides enough is enough.

High Conflict Persons

Sometimes we encounter what Bill Eddy—founder of the High Conflict Institute in San Diego, California, and a top-flight mediator and therapist—calls "high conflict people" (HCPs). Most of us have come into contact with them. According to Eddy, these can be "highly defensive persons who are preoccupied with blaming others and desperate to receive validation for themselves."[3] If you have one or more of these in your family, you know who they are.

---

3. Bill Eddy, *High Conflict People in Legal Disputes* (San Diego: HCI Press, 2005), 24.

Eddy's approach to handling HCPs—whether in a negotiation, at the workplace, or when mediating family matters—is to defuse their defensiveness in order to make progress. One way to do this is to emphasize what he calls "E.A.R." Let's break this down:

> *E* stands for Empathy. When an HCP gets upset, instead of getting angry with them or criticizing their behavior, acknowledge that you know they're upset. Tell them that you empathize with how difficult the situation is for them and that you understand their frustration.

> *A* is for Attention. Here it's important to let them know that you are paying attention to what they're saying and their concerns about an issue.

> *R* is Respect. Make sure they understand that you respect their commitment to solving the problem.[4]

As Bill Eddy points out, applying empathy, attention, and respect doesn't mean you agree, believe what they're saying, or have to listen to them forever. It only means that you are prepared to hear them and work with them toward resolving the issue.

Open-Ended Questions

A good way to begin to listen is to ask open-ended questions, and then be prepared for surprises. It pays to enter a tough conversation with humility, because we often don't know what we don't know. Asking open-ended questions will bring new information and new possibilities for a happy resolution: "How do you see this?" "What do you need?" "Help me understand why _____ is so important to you." "What do you think would be a win-win for everyone?"

An open-ended question is designed to elicit more than a yes or no reply. It usually begins with a "what" or "how" and is designed to keep the conversation going, the flow alive. A close-ended question—one that elicits a yes or no response—limits the information transacted and most likely will result in the conversation

---

4. Eddy, *High Conflict People in Legal Disputes*, 24.

ending, or at least being circumscribed. It can also sound a lot like cross-examination. It's the difference between "How could you help out with Mom?" and "Are you willing to contribute $100 a month to Mom's support?"

Try it out. The next time you're discussing a critical issue, look for opportunities to toss some open questions to your conversation partner. "How did you feel about that?" "What was going through your mind when you heard that?" Rather than "Were you surprised by what you heard?" or "Did you feel angry hearing what she said?" These will only evoke a yes or no and little other information unless the person decides to expand on what they heard.

Be careful of questions that begin with "why." They can risk sounding accusatory, as if you're challenging the responder to justify themselves. Instead of asking "Why didn't you drive Mom to the senior center when you knew she was looking forward to going there?" try "Help me understand your reasons for not taking Mom to the senior center." Or, "I'm not sure I understand your thinking about not taking Mom to the senior center."

Reframing the Issue

The Issue: The question to be decided.

Say you want Mom to move into an attractive assisted living community. She may be set on staying in her home where she's close to friends, doctors, and her church, but you think it's too dangerous for her to be alone. You think the issue is, "How can I get Mom to move?" But if you and Mom together look at her needs (safety, transportation to doctors and grocery stores, daily reminders to take her medicine, and companionship), and your needs (peace of mind, freedom from always being "it" when it comes to driving and errands), you can reframe the issue: "How can Mom stay in her home (or at least in her neighborhood) safely and also give you peace of mind and a clear conscience?"

Once you and Mom agree on the issue, why not continue your conversation another time? Meanwhile, you both can do some research: What services are available in her neighborhood? Can structural changes make the house handicap accessible? How much would they cost? How would they be paid for? What about public programs? Public transportation, taxis, friends, or neighbors who will drive? Devices to call for help in an emergency? Take her to lunch at a nearby senior care residence you think she might like. Explore all the possibilities you both can suggest.

Then you and Mom (and other family members) can decide together on the best path for your particular family. When Sig and I do this exercise in our workshops, participants are astonished. A dozen or more possible solutions may emerge: hiring a health aide who drives; adapting Mom's house to make it more elder-friendly; scheduling family members to check in and help out; daily phone-ins to remind Mom to take her meds; and more.

Even if your first conversation doesn't resolve the issue, it was clearly a success. You agreed on a path forward and have started a process to work through this and other issues that may arise. You listened to each other deeply and treated each other with respect. Each of you felt heard. You took each other's needs and wishes seriously and showed you care about each other. Because of all this, you feel closer than ever, and you're moving ahead together.

Reframing Language

Sometimes, however, tough conversations don't go that smoothly. In such cases, remember that words matter. Calling someone a liar won't get you heard and just might get you punched! Instead of calling the other person a liar, try saying, "I remember that differently." This approach will keep people listening.

In *Crucial Conversations*, the authors say that two things are necessary for people to keep talking: safety and respect.[5] Name-calling is disrespectful and will shut down a conversation or turn it into a shouting match. Bullying, raising voices, finger-pointing, and getting in the other person's face threaten us and send us directly to fight, flight, or paralysis. We don't feel safe.

---

5. Kerry Patterson, Joseph Grenny, Ron McMillan, and Al Switzler, *Crucial Conversations: Tools for Talking When Stakes Are High* (New York: McGraw-Hill, 2002).

What if someone is trying to verbally bully you? Here are some things you can do to stand your ground without getting defensive:

1. Imagine: What's the fear behind the anger? Ask yourself, "What would make me act like that?"

2. Reframe what the person just said in less toxic language. Then answer *that* question. For instance, absent brother shouts, "You're wasting Mom's money! I never could trust you!" Caregiving sister responds, "Sounds like you have questions about Mom's expenses. Would you like to see her checking account statement?"

3. Ask a question. If someone accuses you of lying, ask, "What part of the truth do you think I'm leaving out?"

4. Request clarification. Overstressed caregiver says to sister, "You don't care if I'm dead or alive!" To keep emotions from escalating, sister replies, "Wow. Help me understand what you mean when you say I don't care. Can you give me an example?"

5. Make a personal revelation, followed by a request. "I can't think clearly when someone shouts at me. Could you lower your voice?"

6. Check out the other's assumption, and clarify or reframe what you yourself meant or didn't mean. "When I asked what's happening to Mom's money, I didn't mean I don't trust you. I just want information so I can understand what she needs."

7. If you lost your temper—or regret something in the past that the other holds against you—apologize.

8. Breathe. Ask for a time out. "Could we take five minutes and try to calm down?"

Beware of Trigger Words

As we engage in "The Conversation," remember that every word carries a message, every nuance conveys meanings. Words spoken while on "autopilot" may signal indifference on behalf of the speaker. Every tap on a cell phone while pretending to listen likely communicates lack of interest. Words charged with emotion—double charged with facial and body language—accentuate the speaker's intent for better or for worse.

In a sense, a single word or phrase has the potential to act as a trigger, whether intended or not. The triggers that most concern us as mediators are words that evoke disgust, despair, judgment, fear, or contempt:

- "You *should* have done this."
- "You *could* have said that."
- "He *never* does his share."
- "Why?"
- "Whatever."

These are trigger words that invite defensive reactions and divide rather than unite. Compare, for example, "uncertain" (not a trigger) with "bewildered" and "confused." Or, "dismayed" with "annoyed" and "enraged." Or, "humbled" with "demeaned" and "humiliated." The list goes on and on.

Pronouns matter. In his book *The Dance of Opposites*, author Kenneth Cloke notes that the pronouns we use can provoke ill feeling, if not conflict. Beginning a statement with "you" may unintentionally trigger blame or sound accusatory: "You always want things your way." An alternative approach might be: "I have the sense that you'd rather handle the situation yourself." The pronoun "they" often suggests stereotyping: "They deserve what happened to them." It seems as if what happened to them was likely to occur (because they are not like us?). "He" and "she" may connote demonization or disgrace. "She's wrong as usual." Or, "He's as irresponsible as his parents." Less judgmental expressions might be: "It's a shame things turned out badly for her." Or, "I see some similarity between his actions and what his parents might have done."

While mediators have to be conscious of every word they utter, the same is true of the rest of us as well. This especially applies to the elderly, who often feel vulnerable as their autonomy shrinks and dependence swells. Avoid "elderspeak," such as calling elders "Honey" or "Sweetie" or by their first names, or talking *about* them instead of *to* them when they're in the room. Triggers can also widen the breach that separates siblings who share responsibility for older parents or relations. Conversely, they can enhance collaboration and mutual respect.

If you feel compelled to express your concern, stop and think about how your words will play out, and reframe them in ways that don't risk alienation but rather encourage support and cooperation. For example, instead of "should-ing" ask an elder whether there is another way she might handle a situation or what she has thought of doing about a matter.

The Power of an "I" Statement

Closely related to the skill of *listening to understand* is *speaking to be heard*. If you want to be listened to and understood, learn to make "I" statements.

An "I" statement has three parts: (1) name a behavior or specific incident, (2) describe how it affected you, and (3) sometimes make a request. Here's an example: "Dad, when you had to go to the ER this week and didn't tell me until later, it really scared me" (not "*you* really scared me"). "I love you. I have your medical power of attorney, and I need to know when you have a medical problem. Will you promise to call me next time, right after you call 911?" Inserting the word "I" into the message defuses the exchange by replacing what sounds like blame or an accusation with a feeling for which you take responsibility.

In July 2013, after the acquittal of George Zimmerman in the killing of Trayvon Martin, an unarmed black teenager, President Obama spoke informally without teleprompters or script at a surprise press conference. The president addressed two audiences. He wanted white people to understand why black people felt so strongly that the verdict was unfair. And he wanted black people to know he really did understand, because "I could have been Trayvon Martin." The president never mentioned the word *anger*. Instead, he spoke about pain. He didn't label anyone a racist or criticize the jury's verdict. He talked about "lived" experiences—his own and those of others—of growing up black and male in America. Being followed in department stores. Seeing women hold their breath and clutch their purses when he got on an elevator. Hearing the "click" of car door locks as he approached.

Obama's talk was a perfect example of an "I" message: he named what happened, how it affected him emotionally, and why. One simply talks about one's own experience and emotions. No name-calling, no blame, no threats.

An "I" message doesn't frighten the other party or put them on the defensive. It allows the other person to really hear, to make a heart connection, and to arouse compassion. The aim of an "I" message is not to prove the other person wrong but to build deeper understanding. An "I" message—whether about race or any other hot-button topic—invites genuine conversation, not debate. It creates a safe space to share mutual vulnerabilities. It's hard to argue with someone else's pain, and hearing it makes it easier to open up about your own. This is one way—a very good way—for reconciliation to begin.

Unintended Consequences

Tough conversations can have unexpected (even positive) outcomes. Take my friend Jan. Her eighty-five-year-old mother, Florence, was hospitalized for three weeks. Florence was miserable. Her doctors couldn't pinpoint the cause of her illness, which was a frustrating and debilitating experience.

Florence was usually pleasant to everyone, and she continued to treat her doctors and senior staff with respect. But she was downright rude to the orderlies and night staff who cared for her. Jan was shocked when she heard Florence ordering them around and even calling them names such as "jerk" and "dumb."

After describing the situation with family members, Jan knew she had to act. It took courage. Jan is the youngest of three and often intimated by Florence. But things had gone too far. After hearing her mother chew out an orderly, Jan said, "Mom! You can't talk that way to people! That's so inappropriate!" (An "I" message might have been more effective: "Mom, I feel embarrassed when you talk that way.") Florence denied ever talking rudely to anyone on the hospital staff. It was as if Jan and her mother were in two different realities, and Jan had little hope that her mother's disrespectful behavior would change. Nevertheless, when Jan visited several days later, things had changed. Florence was polite to everyone, and there was no more disrespectful language or harsh tone of voice.

The lessons are clear: Despite whatever doubts you may have about the outcome of a tough conversation, go for it (even if you don't remember "reframing" or "I messages"!). Be prepared for anything—even a positive result!

How a Mediator Can Help

What happens when you and another person are deadlocked and unable to reach an agreement? A neutral third party (a pastor, trusted cousin, or professional mediator) is often better than going it alone. If you decide to engage in mediation, it's critical to include everyone involved in the issue—the parent(s), if they have sufficient competency to take part, and *all* the siblings, at least by phone. Excluding family members could wreck any agreement coming out of the mediation process.

While mediators don't give legal advice, we do encourage parties to consult with an attorney if they have legal questions. (Attorneys may attend, but we recommend that they let their client speak.) Mediation is confidential, and we ask parties to agree to that in writing. Should the parties wind up in court, mediators cannot be called to testify.

The parties in the case are the decision-makers. Our role is to ensure that everyone has an opportunity to share their concerns and to listen to others taking part. Our charge is to keep the process future-focused; there is nothing we can do to resolve what's already taken place. Finally, we are more interested in the parties' interests and concerns than their positions on the matter.

When everyone agrees on what the issues are, then we can move toward resolving them. And once they're resolved, we can encourage participants to collaborate on carrying out what's been agreed to. In this way, they move from being adversaries to becoming a team.

Out of frustration, however, sometimes one family member will file a lawsuit. This may occasionally be necessary, but it should be a last resort. Mediation is almost always faster, less expensive, and more conciliatory. In mediation there are no winners and losers; the goal is to find a win-win outcome. Moreover, participants control the outcome instead of a judge who has no stake in preserving a family.

Mediation is also more creative. Usually a judge is confined to awarding money that must be paid immediately or to naming a guardian or trustee. Mediation makes space for apology and forgiveness, for "sweat equity" (payment in the form of services) or a payment schedule, for power sharing or a plan for ongoing access to information. The list of possibilities is as long as the imagination of the people involved.

Carolyn once mediated a case that literally would have required at least four separate lawsuits to resolve. Two daughters sued their eighty-two-year-old father for failing to set up a trust for them mandated by their grandfather's will. He'd spent their money instead on his new wife. The daughters also planned to sue their stepmom for unjust enrichment. She, on the other hand, was preparing to file for divorce, alimony, and enforcement of a prenuptial agreement. She claimed he deceived her about the children's money, making her believe he was richer than he was. He threatened to counter-claim for repayment of a $300,000 "loan" he'd given her to buy a beach house in her own name.

After all this, the father's only real asset was a half-interest in the marital home. It was likely nobody would get what they wanted in a court. With Carolyn's help involving, among other things, title transfers, secured loans, and a cash payout from mortgaging the marital home, the parties devised a creative plan to give everybody substantially what they wanted. Moreover, the mortified father apologized to everyone, and his daughters at least forgave him. Mediation doesn't always work that well, but when it does the results can seem miraculous.

Breaking through an Impasse

But what if neither side will give? Here are some ways to resolve a dispute—or at least minimize your differences:

1. Take a break. Breathe. Take ten minutes, ten hours, or ten days—however long it takes to cool down tensions between you and the other party.

2. Let the other side save face. Don't try to force the other to admit they're wrong. You may both be right *and* wrong! Show some humility. Say, "I may be wrong, but here's how I see it." Alternatively, sometimes offering to keep a discussion confidential is enough to move forward.

3. Is an apology needed? Or its flip side, forgiveness? This takes courage but is a magic key to reconciliation.

4. New information may unfreeze a stalemate. Perhaps you and a parent are deadlocked over whether he or she should continue driving. Learning that a local organization provides free rides may diminish or even evaporate resistance.

5. Reality check. If two siblings are at odds over the value of a vacation home, or the family home, or an heirloom, get an appraisal. Learning the facts may cool down passions. Before an issue boils over, call in a neutral expert.

6. Discuss the possible downsides of not reaching agreement. Will you end up in litigation with its costs, stress, delay, and irrevocable bad feelings?

7. Stop. Return to the beginning. Review the areas where you do agree. Look for commonalities. Express appreciation for the other. Then see whether those areas of agreement open new paths to resolution.

8. Brainstorm. You may be stuck in a box. Take a moment to fire away with as many out-of-the-box options for settlement as you can. The key to successful brainstorming is *not* to critique each other's suggestions while they're going up on the board. Wait until each has exhausted their storehouse of possibilities. Then try to come up with the best two or three and work down from there.

9. Collaborate. This is the most important technique of all. Shift your goal from winning to finding an answer together that meets everyone's needs.

10. When a discussion with someone near and dear can't get past an impasse, it may be time to drop the topic (at least temporarily) and detour around the mountain. The point is to find a way to demonstrate that the relationship is more important than winning an argument, even a serious one. Take time to breathe, lower your voice, and work on your friendship.

Humor

When a conversation gets tense or goes silent, a little levity can do wonders. President Ronald Reagan, the "Great Communicator," was a master at this. One of his finest performances occurred in the operating room of George Washington University Hospital on March 30, 1981. He'd been shot, and doctors were desperately trying to stop his massive internal bleeding. He'd already had four transfusions and lost half his own blood.

A team of surgeons was preparing to anesthetize him so they could open his chest, repair the damage, and retrieve an attempted assassin's bullet. There was great doubt he would survive. Their hands were shaking. They were about to cut open the president of the United States!

Quite unexpectedly in the operating room, Reagan raised himself up on one elbow, moved his oxygen mask so he could speak, and said, "I hope you're all Republicans." The unbearable tension was broken as they burst out laughing. Dr. Benjamin Aaron, a liberal Democrat, assured him, "Today, Mr. President, we're all Republicans."[6]

Humor can also help in ordinary arguments. A fellow mediator tells this story: She was getting nowhere with two parties, who kept insisting "I want this" and "I want that." No one would move. Annoyed, she said, "Well, I want George Clooney naked on a beach, but we don't always get what we want!" That cleared the air!

A couple of things to note: the butt of the joke should be the teller, not the listener. That's obviously true of the second

---

6. This story has been told in many places. See, for example, Jerry and Carolyn Parr, *In the Secret Service: The True Story of the Man Who Saved President Reagan's Life* (London: Tyndale Press, 2013), 223; see also 232.

joke. But even Reagan's comment was self-deprecating in that he acknowledged—in jest, but with a tinge of reality—his own fear and insecurity. The second point is that it allows everyone in the room to recognize their common humanity. Not only is my opponent laughing, but so am I. Both of us may be unrealistic to think we can always get our way—or, in Reagan's case, that we're all Republicans. He made the point that we're all vulnerable human beings whose deepest need in distress is compassion and care. We're all in this together. Breaking the tension with humor opens everyone's field of focus. It helps the parties move from fear and defensiveness to creativity, from competition to collaboration.

Reprise: Roy and Elizabeth's Story

They did reach a solution, of sorts, but it wasn't what the children had hoped: They opted for autonomy at the price of safety. As competent adults, this was their choice and their children respected it. After two more strokes for Roy and a fall and broken arm for Elizabeth, they are still firmly in their apartment. They remain unwilling to engage in "The Conversation." Their kids continue to love them and worry about them. Elizabeth still goes to work every day, and Roy is still at home alone. He doesn't complain. He loves his wife, is proud of her, and wants her to be happy. The children accept this. They have done what they could, and now they must step back. The family love is still flowing, and that may be the best result possible.

4

Dumb (and Dangerous) Assumptions

by Carolyn

On September 11, 2001, my husband Jerry and I arrived in Shannon, Ireland, just a couple of hours before the planes hit the Twin Towers in New York. The next day, like everyone else on our tour, I was still in shock.

In the restroom of the pub where I stopped, the only other occupant was a teenager, red hair in spikes, lots of piercings, and a few tattoos. I looked away, certain she wouldn't want to speak to me. But she approached and asked, "Are you an American?" When I nodded, she came over and put her arms around me and said, "I'm so sorry about what happened."

For the first time since I heard the news, I was able to weep. That Irish girl's care for me was both a gift and a surprise. I'd dismissed her, assuming we had nothing in common. But I was wrong. We shared our simple humanity. She was, in fact, an agent of love.

Check It Out

We all do it. We can't seem to help it. We make assumptions when we believe something to be true without proof, or we take something for granted. Assumptions are dangerous, because they may be unfair and wrong.

We tend to judge events and people based on our experiences. This can be useful as a shortcut when a situation is either unimportant or requires a quick decision. But often, assumptions reinforce misunderstandings and lead to conflict. Some common types of assumptions are labeling, fortune-telling, mind reading, and "should-ing":

- *Labeling:* "He's sloppy. You're lazy. She's disorganized. I'm stupid." Labels limit us and others. They reinforce negative stereotypes, discourage growth, and limit our ability to think creatively. I'd thought a tattooed, pierced Irish girl would not care a fig about a middle-aged American. I was wrong.

- *Fortune-Telling:* "He won't carry through on his commitments." "If I say anything, she'll get mad." "If I let her do this, she'll mess up." Fortune-telling sets negative goals and then lives down to them. It can be a self-fulfilling prophecy and an excuse for not trying.

The two types I most often encounter in others and in myself, however, are mind reading and "should-ing."

Mind Reading

"She doesn't understand how hard this is." "He doesn't care about my feelings." "They don't really want to help out. All they want is money."

We presume we know what the other person thinks and ignore evidence that might tell us something more positive. If we act on this without checking, then we limit our opportunity to understand and the other person's ability to change.

The other side of mind reading is demanding that others read *my* mind.

Have you ever had a friend or family member withdraw or become angry and you had no clue why? The answer may be simple: you failed to read his/her mind! This can become especially acute around the holidays. Gift giving can be a minefield.

If you ask your sister what she'd like for Christmas or Hanukkah, she may respond in any of several ways. She gives you a list, without saying "choose one" (um, does this mean she expects everything on the list, or she just wants to keep an element of surprise?). If you choose wrong, she may be disappointed. If you buy everything, she may scold you for being extravagant and/or making her look bad because she gave you only one present. Or the items may be of varying prices. Will she be disappointed if you don't buy the most expensive? Will you look cheap?

Or Dad may say, "Really, I have everything I need. You don't have to give me anything." He does have everything he needs. But still, he really does expect something. At least make him some cookies, or give a gift to his favorite charity in his honor. Mind reading is a type of assumption based on expectation. If we fail to do it correctly, we can be punished.

Carolyn Hax, advice columnist for *The Washington Post*, often discusses the differing meanings put on an engagement ring. Should the recipient have a voice in choosing it? Is it a simple expression of love, an investment, a symbol of ownership, a piece of jewelry the woman is expected to wear the rest of her life, a status symbol, or all of the above? Unconscious (and unmatched) assumptions leave a lot of room for disappointment to both giver and recipient. She also tackles mind reading about birthdays. Big deal or no big deal?[1] To avoid disappointment about unmet expectations, Hax encourages readers to examine their unconscious assumptions about holidays and gift giving (including dollar expectations) ahead of time and talk about this with their partner or spouse. If they're disappointed after the fact, then they should take responsibility for their own lack of communication and let it go.

"Should-ing"

Grandmothers should babysit their grandchildren. Women shouldn't have careers. Men shouldn't cry. Daughters should take care of elderly parents. The oldest child should be the executor of the will. Right?

"Shoulds" come from being stuck in a pattern of "how it's supposed to be," based on cultural assumptions and our own limited experience or on other people's expectations. They can lead to guilt and judging, rather than to creating new possibilities.

---

1. For example, see https://www.washingtonpost.com/lifestyle/style /carolyn-hax-boyfriend-comes-through-after-girlfriend-drops-hints /2015/06/19/155cd782-095d-11e5-9e39-0db921c47b93_story.html?utm _term=.95a81296fff7.

A lot of suffering is caused by trying to live up to someone's ideal of how "it ought to be" or expecting them to conform to your model. Someone once said, "The perfect is the enemy of the good." We all know in our heads that there's no such thing as perfection, yet we insist on it from others. This can be especially true in families, where we really ought to know better. Many difficult conversations would be easier if we could value authenticity and drop the expectations that others can't (or won't) meet.

Joanna asked her siblings to contribute $50 a month toward the expenses of their ninety-year-old parents who were living with her. The siblings lived far away and could not give any of their time, so Joanna thought that request was perfectly reasonable. They, however, disagreed. Her brother asked, "Why are *you* asking *me* for money? You have more money than I do!" The sister grudgingly agreed to contribute, but demanded a full accounting each month of how the $50 was spent. "How can I be sure it's going to Mom and Dad and not to clean *your* part of the house or wash *your* clothes?"

Joanna was stunned. Her siblings were employed. They had no children at home. They owned homes. They were not poor. Joanna had a demanding job, was spending much more than $50 monthly on her parents' needs, and she wanted to hire a cleaning lady once a week to help out. She thought, "Adult kids should want to contribute to their parents' well-being. They should appreciate what I'm doing and want to help! Don't they care about Mom and Dad? Don't they care for me?"

Her "shoulds" were reasonable. For a brief time she was so hurt she considered cutting off all communication. But after weighing the cost of a family rupture and how it would affect her mother and father, she made a conscious decision to forgive and move on. Each sibling did come to visit the parents once a year for a week, so Joanna and her husband could take a little vacation. It wasn't all she wanted, but she appreciated the break and decided it had to be good enough.

It's not only siblings. Sometimes we nurture old resentments against Mom or Dad because of "how it should have been" but wasn't. Rehearsing old hurts with a less than perfect parent who now has dementia or cancer is not only futile—it's cruel and exhausting. When I think about how many mistakes I've made with my own kids, it's easier to forgive my parents' failures. They wanted to be good parents. *And they were good enough.*

I'm working on letting go of my ideas of how other people should behave. It's a work in progress and it's not easy. But I want to see their real beauty as they are and love them, warts and all. I want to find their faults endearing or, as my husband likes to say to young couples he's about to marry, "You have to learn to trivialize each other's idiosyncrasies."

"Say What?"

Even friendly assumptions can lead to frustrating miscommunications.

Picture this: Years ago, I was at the check-in counter in Rome's Fumicino Airport with my husband Jerry. In trying to be helpful, the ticket agent offered to change our seats in Economy Plus so we could sit together. "You'll be in the center section."

"No, thank you," I said. "Right now we have one aisle seat and one on the bulkhead row. We'll keep the ones we have."

"But you're not together," she patiently explained. "I'll put you together," she said, typing into her computer.

I felt a surge of anxiety. Jerry was six-foot tall and needed legroom. I was (and still am) slightly claustrophobic. We didn't want to be crammed in the middle section.

I tried again, "We'd rather keep the seats we have. Please don't change anything." She looked at me as if I were a preverbal child. She slowly, patiently, repeated herself. "You . . . are . . . not . . . sitting . . . together. I will put you together."

I heard then what my husband used to describe as "an edge" in my voice. "*We prefer to keep the seats we have!*" She shrugged and surrendered. Finally.

What was there not to understand? I gave her a very clear message, but her friendly assumption got in the way. She saw an older couple, obviously affectionate, and assumed we would want to sit together. What she did not "get" was that at that point we had been sitting together for fifty-one years and hoped to have many more

opportunities to do so. But on a nine-hour flight, each of us preferred to be able to get in and out without a lot of rigmarole. Men of
a certain age need to go to the bathroom more often than younger
folks. I feel very uncomfortable if I cannot see a clear path of egress
from some direction (an aisle or up front). We both were subject to
leg cramps and needed to be able to stretch and move our legs and
feet. But I didn't want to have to share our history with the agent; I
just wanted to keep the seats we already had.

The message here is this: When a conversation begins to re-
cycle itself, check your assumptions and those of the other person.
She might have simply confirmed that she'd heard me correctly.
"You'd prefer to keep the seats you have?" would have worked. On
the other hand, I could have thanked her for her thoughtfulness
and mentioned our need to stretch. Maybe I lost an opportunity
to affirm her sense of concern for older passengers *and still keep
our seats.*

Looking at What You Don't Know

Most assumptions are unconscious or deeply embedded in our
culture. ("Old people can't manage their own lives.") So how do I
bring them to awareness? How do I identify my own?

Usually, we know what we know. I know how to make mac
and cheese. We know what we don't know. I don't speak Swahili.
The tricky part is hidden in a box we might label "What I don't
know that I don't know." That's where assumptions live. That box
is dangerous.

In human relations, we get into trouble when we are blind to
a hole in our thinking. How can you find out there's a hole in your
thinking? Ask yourself questions. Here's an example.

Your unemployed bachelor brother Jim has moved in with
Mom. You're convinced he's taking advantage of her. *Why doesn't
he get a job like a normal person?* This whole situation really ticks
you off!

But before you climb down Jim's throat, let's take a look at what
you don't know. One way is to begin questions with "might." Turn
your imagination loose:

- Might Jim be actively looking for work?

- Could he be giving Mom something from his unemployment check?

- Does Mom welcome Jim's presence? Might she be really lonely by herself?

- Is Jim making personal sacrifices to take care of Mom? Does he have a girlfriend he's neglecting? Is he able to maintain any social life of his own?

- Is Jim doing household chores and repairs that Mom would have to pay someone else to do? How much might that be worth?

- What personal care does Mom require? Have I asked lately? What would such care cost? Might Jim actually be saving Mom money?

Once you discover the holes in your thinking (what you didn't know that you didn't know), then you can ask questions and get answers. That makes it a lot easier to get on the same page with the people you love.

Need to Be Right and Righteous? Give It Up!

Picture an extended family gathered for a Thanksgiving feast, and the following happens:

- A granddaughter announces she's moving in with her boyfriend.

- A son has brought his same-sex partner to meet the family.

- You learn your favorite cousin had an abortion.

- The family vegetarian ostentatiously declines the turkey and anything it touched.

- Your mom's friend who helped make dinner is a guy ten years younger than she and you suspect he's more than a "friend."

- A Marine in uniform and a peace activist complete the scene.

(I'm only partially making this up. I've seen each of these situations—but, I confess, never all at once!)

The need to be right and righteous can derail family relationships quicker than anything else, sometimes forever. When someone says "It's a matter of principle" or starts quoting Scripture to buttress a position, or refers to those who disagree as "evil," it's time to pass the Pepto-Bismol.

What's wrong with wanting to be right? And good? Nothing, if we are able to swallow a large dose of humility with our turkey and allow that *we may be wrong.* Or, more realistically, we may be partly right and partly wrong. And partly blind. Common ground and common values can be found in the midst of so much diversity. We just have to be willing to focus on the big picture.

So what can this family talk about? *Anything they want to, if they keep their vision large enough.* They may still share common values: a yearning to give and receive love, kindness to animals, a safe world in which to bring up children, respect for human life. There are many ways to express these values. Some are represented at the table; others haven't yet been dreamed. Rumi, a twelfth-century Persian poet, said it this way: "Out beyond ideas of wrong-doing and right-doing there is a field. I will meet you there."

How to Find the "Field": Ask for Directions

The map to Rumi's field can be discovered by being brave enough to ask the right questions.

When Sig and his wife Susan celebrated a significant wedding anniversary with their faith community, Sig spoke on a reading from Genesis 40 in the Hebrew Bible. It's the scene where Joseph, who had been unjustly imprisoned, noticed that two fellow prisoners seem troubled and asked them, "Why are your faces downcast today?" This question opened a conversation that resulted in Joseph's being freed, becoming the most powerful man in Egypt under Pharaoh, and changing the course of history.

Sig's point: It can be more helpful to notice another's body language and ask the right questions than to have the right answers. This creates trust that helps couples build enduring marriages like Sig and Susan's. Empathetic questions are tools that smooth workplace relationships, cross generational divides, and help to heal old wounds.

What kinds of questions do this? Questions that are open—we don't know the answer—and that show interest without prying (see chapter 3). They respect the other's dignity and boundaries. They are not judgmental. They invite a real exchange, in as much depth as the other senses is comfortable and safe. They signal that you want to hear the other's story in as much richness of emotion and detail as they want to share. And they don't insist.

Opportunities abound daily to practice this healing act, *if* we're willing to engage.

- Young friends do it without thinking. "¿Qué pasa?" "What's up?"
- Elder friends do it with each other. "How's your spirit?"
- Coworkers do it. "What are you working on these days?"
- Couples do it. "Honey, you seem cheerful. Did something good happen today?"
- Happy families do it. "Mom, how was it for you when Dad was transferred to New York?"
- Strangers do it. "What brings you to this meeting?" "What do you think about [current events] . . . ?"

An open question can't be answered with one word. You'll know you've asked a good one when you get a response to which your next words are "Tell me more."

The Role of Doubt

The Marx Brothers had a comedy routine where a wife encounters her husband with another woman. Surprised, he looks up and says, "Who do you trust? Me or your lying eyes?"

There are grounds to actually doubt not only our assumptions but even our own eyewitness memory of a traumatic incident. Terrible things can happen when we're sure that we're right, but we're really wrong. Desdemona did not cheat on Othello. Juliet was not really dead.

According to *The Washington Lawyer*, since 1989, DNA evidence has exonerated 506 innocent people convicted of serious felonies based on eyewitness testimony.[2] The witnesses believed

---

2. See also this story in *The New Yorker*, http://www.newyorker.com /magazine/2015/04/13/the-price-of-a-life.

their memories were accurate. They were wrong. It's tragic when an innocent person is sent to prison. It's also tragic when a family is destroyed because brothers and sisters (or parents) remember an upsetting event differently and blame one another. Each is certain that his or her memory is not only true, but the only version possible. How does this happen? Why does this happen?

Author Sarah Kellogg explains that memory "tends to focus more on unpleasant experiences as a way to . . . be better prepared for the next looming encounter."[3] Kellogg writes that memory also focuses on the senses and emotions rather than the intellect, so important facts are not noted. A crime victim may notice how the perpetrator smelled or his strength, but not his age or height or weight. Sequence may also be missed.

A family member might focus on an insult, forgetting completely what happened beforehand that triggered the event (more about this in chapter 5). As a former judge, I know this to be true: differing witnesses can be absolutely certain they are telling the truth—and still be wrong. Before I rush to call another person a liar because her memory of a traumatic event is different from mine, I need to hear her explanation and understand her perception. I need to look at other evidence, and I need to check out other people's memories. And I need to have a little more humility.

But what difference does all this make ultimately? In human relations—as opposed to criminal trials—establishing the facts is less important than healing the feelings. With rare exceptions, we may never be able to correctly place blame for a rupture completely on one family member. And what good would it do if we could? How much better for a family to hear one another out, to acknowledge that incorrect assumptions may have been made all around, to share responsibility, to express regret, and to jointly decide to turn the page and move on together.

If we want to be remembered as compassionate friends or family members—men or women of justice—then we have to learn to ask the kinds of questions that lead to deeper understanding and trust. And even be willing to question our own memories.

---

3. Sarah Kellogg, "A Flawed Record: The Fragility of Eyewitness Memory," *The Washington Lawyer*, November 2014.

Paradox, Ambiguity, and Enlarging the Box

Experience teaches that truth is not always black and white: life is lived out in shades of gray. True, sometimes we must choose, and sometimes the right path is clear. But when anyone insists "It has to be either/or," pause and ask yourself, "Why? Couldn't it be both/and?"

A paradox is a statement or question that asserts two ideas that seem to be mutually exclusive. The challenge is to find a way to live with both without rejecting either. Can a person be both guilty and not guilty? Can a person of faith both believe and entertain doubt? Can a statement be both true and false? Yes, yes, and yes.

We explain many such situations by saying, "Yes, but . . ." A man is guilty of reckless driving, but he was trying to stop his two-year-old climbing out of the car seat. Mother Theresa devoted her life to dying beggars in Calcutta whom she likened to "Jesus, in his distressing disguise." But at the same time she confessed her doubts in letters to her priest. Yes, teenagers want their parents to leave them alone—but they want them also to be there for support.

Sometimes the tension is overcome by discovering a third way. This is the path of *enlarging the box*. Instead of "yes, but" we say "both/and." Let's look again at the issue of where Mom will live. After his mother falls and breaks a hip, her worried son says, "Mom can't stay in her house because it has stairs." Mom says, "If I move, I'll lose my independence. I'm not moving." Well, let's brainstorm how maybe Mom can stay (and keep her freedom) *and* be safe:

- Get a stair lift
- Transform her dining room into a bedroom
- Add a first-floor addition with a bedroom and bath to her house
- Hire an aide
- All of the above or something else

An ambiguous statement is one that can be interpreted in more than one way. Ambiguities are often deliberately created as ways to resolve or detour around paradoxes. They are popular with government officials who draft treaties and create legislation. Crucial terms may be deliberatively kept vague to allow for interpretation as events unfold. "Due process." "Conduct unbecoming an officer." "Obscenity." "Resisting arrest." Some words are inherently ambiguous: "Justice." "Love." "Beauty."

Paradox and ambiguity are both forms of nondualistic thinking. They open the mind in creative ways. They inhabit a more spacious territory than either/or, black or white. If you can sometimes see the world in shades of gray rather than black and white, then you are thinking nondualistically.

The ability to tolerate ambiguity is a sign of maturity. Even when a paradox seems impossible to reconcile, such as deeply held differing religious or political convictions, people can find a way to connect. Both Pope Francis and the Dalai Lama strike me as nondualistic thinkers. And their presence is almost universally experienced as a blessing.

Thomas Merton noticed that when theologians meet they tend to argue, trying to prove each other wrong; but when Buddhist, Hindu, and Christian contemplatives sit together in silence, they can access a common well of spiritual wisdom. They feel connected to each other in a space larger and deeper than creed or even rationality. They can *allow mystery to be mystery and let the rest go.*

Don't Shoot the Messenger

Warning: If negative assumptions harden and become toxic, you may be asked to carry a message from one family member to another. There are some things you need to consider before you agree.

First, you should entertain healthy doubt that you're getting the full and complete story from either side. When someone tells me about a situation or another person's behavior or actions, my mediator mind automatically responds: "Hm, I wonder if there is another side to this story." Or, "What would the other person say about that?"

It's undeniable that there are almost always at least two sides to every story. When we tell our story, it's commonplace to "cherry-pick" the facts or slant our version to gain our listener's sympathy—

and it's likely the other party is doing the same thing. In fact, both parties may think they're telling the truth. Can there be more than one truth?

When Sig reluctantly agreed to be a go-between (outside a mediation setting), it did not go well. He decided to check with someone who was an expert on bringing messages to opposing parties: the daughter of a divorced couple. The young woman generously shared her five practical rules for transmitting messages in such a delicate case. With her permission, here they are:

1. Prepare to be shot. No matter how hard you try not to be in the line of fire, you will likely become a target.

2. Try to impress on the recipient that you are in no way responsible for the message. Try even though you'll probably fail.

3. Empathize with the recipient. Say, "I can imagine how you must feel, how hard it must be to hear what I have to say."

4. Get ready to listen to the recipient vent. Sadly, your job isn't complete until you have duly heard the recipient blast away at the sender—as well as at yourself.

5. Finally, proclaim your neutrality. Again. It is critical that you repeat that you don't have a dog in this fight.

The best advice Sig has, however, is that unless you're a trained mediator, don't take on the messenger role. The best mediators have the humility to acknowledge that some competing truths simply cannot be logically resolved. We don't have all the answers either.

Essential Assumptions and Recent Events

Finally, it's important to remember that not all assumptions are bad. In fact, some shared assumptions are absolutely crucial to our common survival. The fabric of our human social culture is woven together by trust. When trust is broken, a deep sense of anxiety covers us all like a torn shroud.

On March 24, 2015, copilot Andreas Lubitz, age twenty-seven, deliberately drove Germanwings Flight 9525 into the French Alps, killing all 149 passengers and himself. Life together in organized society requires that we put our lives in the hands of strangers. When we get on a plane, we believe the pilot wants to land it safely.

I trust that my doctor actually earned an MD, is legally licensed to treat me, and wants me to heal. I trust that my child's teacher knows her subject and is kind to children. I expect the police officer who stops me to give me a ticket, but I don't expect to be shot. Even if these assumptions prove incorrect and people are hurt (or killed), we have no choice but to continue to assume the best. As Job said, surrendering to the will of God, "Though he slay me, yet will I trust him."

This trust is necessary. We are not on our own and could not survive for long if we were. *Even when trust is broken, we must continue to trust.* I will continue to fly, even though I may feel a fear I did not previously entertain. If a teacher is incompetent, I'll complain and try to get him or her removed, but I'll continue to send my child to school. I will continue to see doctors without checking their credentials first. I'll continue to call 911 in a crisis but will hold police and firefighters accountable. If something seems amiss, I hope that now I'll ask more questions or complain more loudly. But I have to continue to trust. I have no choice.

And we must look out for one another other. As the DC Metro system continuously announces, "If you see something, say something." In a weird way, stories of police who shoot unarmed protesters or other innocent citizens, or physicians who deliberately harm patients, or beloved role-model comedians who allegedly drug and rape their admirers, or priests who betray children, or pilots who drive a passenger jet into the French Alps—these stories have the power to bring us together. They illustrate our common need for safety, our need to take responsibility for one another. Now I am more strongly committed to come to another's aid when that person is in danger. And I will march in the streets if need be to hold wrongdoers accountable.

There are some assumptions we must fight to protect, so that we and our children will not only survive but prevail. Other assumptions may need closer scrutiny, however, and nowhere is that more important than with relations among siblings.

5

Siblings in War and Peace

by Sig and Carolyn

"When we have no peace,
it's because we've forgotten we belong to each other."

Mother Teresa

You may remember a touching logo from Father Flanagan's Boys Town in Nebraska. It shows a kid about ten years old carrying a younger child on his back. He says to the priest, "He ain't heavy, Father. He's my brother."

Would that it were so! But from biblical times to the present, sibling rivalry has been as common as sibling love. Adam and Eve had two sons, Cain and Abel, until Cain murdered his brother because of jealousy. Jacob colluded with his mother, who favored him, to deceive his blind old father and rob his twin brother, Esau, of his birthright. It ran in the family: Jacob's own sons sold Joseph, his favorite, into slavery and told their father that a wild animal ate him (more about that later). Experience teaches that siblings can indeed be heavy—to the point where one may even wish the other dead.

Carolyn Hax, the advice columnist mentioned earlier, published a story in which a reader describes being shunned by her siblings after their parents died; they even told a judge there were no other children. The shunned child had to go to court to prove she existed![1]

Carolyn (Parr) mediated a case where a probate judge in the DC Superior Court, fed up with a squabble over whether a Vietnamese

---

1. Carolyn Hax, "Don't Leave Family Conflicts Unaddressed," *The Washington Post*, March 21, 2015.

woman living abroad was really the American father's biological child (as three of the four US siblings agreed), got thoroughly fed up. The judge ended the squabble by ordering the father's body exhumed to extract his DNA (we'll share the rest of this story later).

When we tell people that we mediate disputes in adult families, listeners often volunteer their own stories, usually with siblings in a starring role. Like sour cream, the family dysfunction rises to the top and curdles upon the death of a parent.

Norma's story is not unusual. "The first thing I did when my mother died was change the locks on her home."

"Why?" Sig asked.

"I didn't want my greedy older brother rummaging through Mom's home until her will was read and we all learned who was getting what. And I was right. No sooner had I changed the locks than he called from Mom's front door, furious that he couldn't get in."

Sig makes no judgment as to whether Norma was justified or unduly suspicious. The only point is that she felt she had to do what she did.

Beware of the "Swooper"

Then there's the "swooper," as depicted in the following story. Bert, a volunteer at the soup kitchen where Sig helps out, had been his mother's primary caregiver for nine years until she died.

"Any siblings?" Sig asked.

"Yeah. Three."

"What did they do to help?"

"Well, one sister was going through tough times of her own and could only give a hand once in a while. My youngest sister was away at college. Our brother Eric lives in Richmond, about seventy miles from here. But when he visited once a month, there was hell to pay."

Bert thought he and a part-time aide had done a pretty good job of caring for his mother. But Eric is a "swooper"—a relative who lives out of town and periodically "swoops in" to check up on the parents and caregivers.

Some swoopers see the glass half empty. They are ready to pounce on any perceived laxity and dictate all kinds of changes in the care plan. This results in caregivers feeling defensive. Once a swooper has created enough chaos (in the eyes of the local caregivers), they depart the scene, leaving those behind to pick up the pieces.

If you have any swoopers in your family, how do you deal with them?

- First, humble yourself and listen to their suggestions. Most swoopers' primary concern is the well-being of the ailing relative or parent. They may have some good ideas, and they may really just want to be helpful.

- Understand that because they live out of town, they may wrestle with the guilt that comes with not being on the scene. Try to look beyond the words and feel a little empathy.

- Suggest specific ways they can help. Is there something they could send to your parent? More frequent phone calls? How about taking Dad for a weekend or coming to free you up for a break? Let yourself be surprised by a positive response.

- Keep the channels of communication open. Swoopers can experience extreme anxiety because of distance. Perhaps sharing information with them more frequently via phone or e-mail can alleviate their concerns.

- If these suggestions don't work, then call a family meeting (if possible, with the parents present) and with someone familiar with the parents' medical condition, such as a geriatric care specialist. Try to design a care plan that out-of-town siblings feel comfortable with and that alleviates their concerns.

Bert went on to say that he had inherited half his mother's home. What about the other half? It was divided among the other siblings. Sig silently cringed. There may have been better ways to reward Bert for his nine years of special attention, especially if Mom wanted him to be able to live in the house. At the very least, she should have made clear to the other children that this unequal distribution was not because she loved them less.

Bert's brother recently hired an attorney to help him claim the entire home. He may lose on that, but he will probably be able to force a sale and division of the proceeds.

The Toxic Triangle

Sibling resentment begins in childhood, when a parent appears to favor one child over another. When this happens, a toxic triangle is formed between the parent, the favored child, and the disfavored child. The disfavored child will continue to long for the parent's love and approval but may grow to hate the favored child. The favored child may revel in the parent's attention but may not have done anything to cause the favoritism.

In his book *The Sibling Effect*, author Jeffrey Kluger writes, "No matter the gender, era, or temperaments of any adult sibling group, nothing will test their relationships quite as much as the challenge of tending to aging parents."[2] Kluger also notes that the oldest child is most likely to take responsibility, the middle child contributes, and the youngest often does the least. (Our own mediation cases have not backed this up. We've had several cases where the youngest child assumed the heaviest load.)

Let's return to the biblical account of Joseph for a moment. Carolyn took her granddaughter Ellie to see Andrew Lloyd Weber's *Joseph and the Amazing Technicolor Dreamcoat*, a lighthearted musical retelling of the story found in Genesis 37. Joseph was the second youngest of Jacob's twelve sons, and the one most dearly loved. He was thrilled with Dad's gift of a "coat of many colors." Then he dreamed that his brothers would bow down to him—and he was dumb enough to tell them that! His sense of entitlement evoked his brothers' hatred and they subsequently sold him into slavery.

After the show, Carolyn asked Ellie, "Do you think the brothers did a bad thing?"

"Yes," she said. "But Joseph shouldn't have bragged." Then she added, "But it was really their father's fault."

Ellie had it right: As a teenager, Joseph was too naive to know how to neutralize his adult brothers' jealousy. Jacob loved Joseph more than his other sons because his mother was Rachel, Jacob's favorite wife, who had died giving birth to their second son, Ben-

---

2. Jeffrey Kluger, *The Sibling Effect: What the Bonds among Brothers and Sisters Reveal about Us* (New York: Riverhead Books, 2011), 280–81.

jamin. While Joseph's birth was celebrated, Benjamin's was grieved. Jacob apparently took his other sons for granted, but Joseph did not choose his mother or his own birth order. In addition, two of Jacob's older sons had murdered members of a local tribe that was suing for peace. Those brothers brought shame on Jacob, who had to flee with the family. Their father therefore had reason to think less of them.

Joseph's brothers should have been held accountable for their actions. And true, Joseph should not have flaunted his favored status. But *most of all*, Jacob should have realized that his actions were hurting all his children.

How does the Joseph story compare with what many families confront today? Older children are often viewed as able to take care of themselves, while younger ones are babied by parents and (too often) bullied by older siblings. As with Jacob's older sons, sometimes a child's own behavior or unwise personal choices lie behind their parent's disfavor. Oddly, disfavored children seldom blame their parents. They want to believe their parents loved them. They can't bear to wonder, "Did I deserve this?" So they blame the "favored" one.

Here's another example: A friend told Sig how his grandmother— thinking she was doing the "right thing"—bequeathed unequal amounts to her three adult children. Mind you, she did not have a large estate. Nevertheless, her will's instructions left a permanent mark on her children's relationships.

To her son who was struggling to keep the family business alive, she left the most. To her daughter who was in fairly good financial shape, she left a "decent" amount. But to her youngest daughter who "married rich," she left the least. The outcome? The daughter who married rich had little or nothing to do with her brother for the rest of their lives.

It wasn't her brother's fault. But that's not how the daughter in question saw things. Had there been some discussion among the grandmother and her children before she finalized her will, the outcome might have been different. This is but one argument in support of family transparency.

In our adult family mediations, we see plenty of sibling resentment:

- "You forged Dad's name on the title!"
- "We know Mom had a will, and you destroyed it."
- "You spent Mom's money on yourself."
- "You turned Mom against me."

Sometimes these accusations are true; often they are not. But almost always, a parent's favoritism (conscious or unconscious) is the root cause of sibling anger. At the least provocation, it can come back to bite them.

Breaking the Triangle

The bad news is that the toxic triangle may continue to define the family dynamics into adulthood. Why can't they get along? What's really going on here?

This triangle bears a resemblance to the Karpman Triangle, known in the field of pop psychology as Transactional Analysis. In his book *A Game Free Life*, Stephen B. Karpman, MD, describes a common pattern found in drama and in everyday life. The triangle consists of a Victim, a Persecutor, and a Rescuer.[3]

A person most often enters the triangle as Rescuer to come to the aid of the perceived victim (think of Mom defending her favorite child); but the Rescuer may soon find herself being attacked either by the Persecutor (and thus becoming a victim herself) or the Victim who rejects her help. She fights back and becomes the Persecutor. Soon everyone is trapped in the triangle, moving from one role to another in an endless cycle, feeling both persecuted and justified.

It's painful and destructive. So why don't they just stop? According to Karpman, they keep "playing the game" because each unconsciously derives a psychic reward. The Rescuer thinks, "I'm good." The Persecutor thinks, "I'm right." The Victim thinks, "I'm blameless."

The good news is that the game ends whenever any player stops playing!

---

3. Stephen B. Karpman, *A Game Free Life* (San Francisco: Drama Triangle Publications, 2014).

What the Favored Child Can Do Right Now

First, stop accepting the advantages of the favored child status. Then begin to share information. If your parents have not built in transparency, take your own steps to build trust with your siblings. If you're living with your parents, you could share your plans to get work or help for Mom and Dad. Let siblings know about your own financial situation so they don't make an incorrect assumption that Mom and Dad are supporting you. If your parents are, in fact, paying you, then you should divulge this and tell your siblings what you're doing to earn that money or what your plans are to repay it.

If you hold the power of attorney and are in fact writing checks on your parents' account, ask your parents if you may send your siblings a copy of each month's bank statement or other financial accounting. Let transparency be your guide.

Demonstrate a desire to collaborate. Seek ways your siblings can participate more fully in your parents' lives. This goes beyond money—to time, phone calls, and visits. Offer hospitality and make them feel welcome.

Begin to level the playing field regarding financial benefits. Sometimes one child has been favored with more financial advantages. If you have unpaid loans to parents or to one or more siblings, attend to repaying them and let it be known.

Maybe your college expenses were fully paid while your brother had to work or take loans. Or you went to an Ivy League school while he attended a state university. Maybe you received an expensive wedding, others less so. Although this could have been the result of your parents' changing financial situation, it may still rankle the others. If money resentments are bubbling, acknowledge the benefit you received. Ask your siblings how you might help even things out. Perhaps you could start a college fund for their kids or pay for piano lessons?

What the Disfavored Child Can Do Right Now

First, quit blaming, shaming, or shunning.

When a situation goes sour—at work, in a family, or even in a faith community—we often look for somebody to blame. As voices rise and fingers point, we need to breathe deeply and call a time-out. Why shouldn't we pile on when someone is obviously at fault? Can't we shame the perpetrator into better behavior? And don't we feel so much better when we "clear the air"?

Here's why blaming is not the path to positive change: To begin with, it's the wrong starting place. To improve a relationship, we need to start with ourselves. Years after a fierce argument, one of Carolyn's close relatives stunned her by confessing, "I wanted to apologize, but I couldn't because you were *so angry!*" Carolyn had no idea her self-righteous anger had created a barrier against the apology she longed to hear.

Even if you feel sure you're right and the other is wrong, chances are you both played a role in the dispute. Maybe you simply didn't make your expectations clear. Or you failed to share information. Or you missed clues that the other was unhappy. (Or you got a psychological pay-off from feeling victimized that you didn't recognize until now.) If you begin a tough conversation by acknowledging your own part, then you make it easier for the other to move from defensiveness to collaboration.

A second reason to quit blaming is that you may be making wrong assumptions (remember chapter 4?). We all assume things based on our own experience. Most assumptions are unconscious—we think they are facts. Our worst mistakes are caused by acting on what we *think* we know that's *flat wrong.*

For example, you may be thinking your little brother lied about you or did something else to prejudice your dad against you. But maybe not. He may have been the totally innocent recipient of Dad's affection because he was the better athlete or looked like Dad's favorite relative—or was just the baby—or who knows what. Get over it.

You may be assuming that because your sister is living at home and hasn't found a job, she must be freeloading. And maybe another assumption is at play here: Do you suspect she's taking advantage of your parents, *because you also assume they are too old to be able to make intelligent decisions about their own best interests?* Maybe you and your sister need a conversation. If so, don't accuse. Instead, ask open questions. You need information. You don't need to blame. In fact, you might even discover a reason to express some appreciation!

The third reason to quit blaming is that it never works; it only makes the situation worse. Alcoholics Anonymous groups have a saying: "One definition of insanity is to do the same thing over and over expecting a different result." Blaming is like scolding an alcoholic. You might feel better temporarily, but you won't change their behavior. Blaming will back the other into a corner which they'll defend to the end.

Neither will blaming heal a broken relationship. What works better is to acknowledge your own part, figure out what you don't know, ask open questions—and then listen to the answers.

Once you and your siblings have worked with one another (including each of you looking at your own behavior and possible fault), you might then be ready to make a joint request from your parent. Or, better yet, give this book to everyone in the family!

What a Parent Can Do Right Now

If you are a mom or dad who hopes to be remembered as a parent who loved all his/her children, here's a suggestion: Stop favoring one child over another!

First, create more opportunities for all your children to participate in your care. Unless there's only one child (or only one who is competent), it's unwise for parents to put all responsibility for their well-being and resources into the hands of a single child. If they want to name Willie as personal representative on their will, then they should consider giving Jill their durable power of attorney. If Betsy lives closest, then she might be a good choice for the medical power of attorney.

Second, in a family conference, share your thinking about a living will or advance care plan—how you hope to be cared for when you can no longer care for yourself (more about these documents in chapter 6). These are sensitive discussions, and you may be hesitant to raise them (revisit chapter 3 for ideas and various resources available to you).

And remember: Transparency is essential in making these arrangements. If you don't want your children to feel you're keeping secrets, then you must understand that the final word is yours. It's okay for them to ask questions and express their views, but they must recognize and demonstrate support for your autonomy. Unless you have disabling dementia, you get to control your own life.

It's helpful if all children have the same information. Equal access to Mom and Dad is the goal here. If you do not share power and knowledge among your children, questions like these will arise: *Why does Jack have financial power of attorney? He's the youngest!* Alvin wonders, *Didn't Mom remember I'm a CPA? Why didn't she pick me? Or Jim should not be Mom's agent for health care! He lives three thousand miles away, and I live down the street. That's not convenient!*

If you're the mother in this case, then you know that you had good reasons for your choices as to who will help you with what. Yes, Jack's the youngest, but he has good judgment and he uses the same bank that you do. Jim is a doctor, and you think that other doctors will talk to him candidly. Alvin, the CPA, is too uptight; you love him dearly, but you know he's going to want every little receipt and want you to keep account of everything down to the smallest scrap of paper. The point here is that it's fine for your children to air potential issues and then hear how you respond. It's still your call, but it will be helpful to your children if you can be more transparent with them so they know what you're thinking.

Often one or more of the disgruntled siblings starts looking for examples of malfeasance: *How come the brother with authority over Mom and Dad's finances got a new car on his crummy salary? Why is Sally living in that fancy four-room condo?* If something looks fishy, children should ask their parents in the least accusatory way possible and try to get answers. But they need to remember that it's still their parents' decision.

Third, you need to share information about your health with your children. Under normal circumstances, all kids should have the names and contact information of your doctors and permission to speak with them. You may think you don't want to worry them, but no child wants to be the last to learn their mom or dad has cancer. When one is left in the dark, assumptions sprout like toadstools and suspicion spreads. Our advice to parents is that when you fill out the forms at your doctor's office saying who can receive your information, you should list *all* your children. A good rule of thumb is that if a parent has confided something to one child, then the parent should tell all of them.

Fourth, share time and attention with all of your kids as much as possible. This includes visits, holidays, and vacation time. Of course, those who live closest will see you more often. But you should make an effort to frequently talk with them all. Make it clear to each of them that you are interested in their lives. And also get to know your grandchildren.

Adult families who really want to heal the wounds of a painful history can do it together. But if even one member commits to leaving the toxic triangle, it will end. The psychic pay-offs will stop and space for something new to flourish will magically appear.

That something may begin with an apology.

The Role of Apology

After any one party offers an olive branch and the triangle war ends, then it's time to clean up the battlefield carnage. It's time to say, "I'm sorry."

Some of us find it very, very hard to apologize. This is because a sincere apology requires humility and courage. It requires us to strip away our self-righteousness and pretense that have ill-served us for so long. We can no longer deny or minimize or blame. We have to allow ourselves to become vulnerable, to look into the mirror of another's eyes without blinking.

To be effective, an apology has to be real. We all recognize a pseudo-apology when we hear one. They often come out of the mouths of embarrassed public figures who have been caught dirty. A counterfeit apology is tentative, nonspecific, and shifts blame from the offender to the offended.

"*If* [tentative] *anyone* [lack of specificity] has been offended [passing the action from self to recipient] by *anything* [lack of specificity] I *may* [tentative] have said or done [lack of specificity], I'm sorry." Or "I regret [less than sorry] that some group [talking *about them*, not *to* them] *may have been* offended [but it's not my fault they're so thin-skinned!]." This kind of "apology" won't do. It's less than useless. It's infuriating. It will only inflame the resentment. A good apology does the following:

- Takes personal responsibility
- Names specific behavior
- Acknowledges the harm caused
- Expresses regret
- Offers amends when possible

Most effective is when the person apologizing does so early, does it himself, and tells it all. And late is better than never. The deepest healing happens when all players do it, because each family member has played a role in creating (and perpetuating) sibling rivalry, even if it was totally unconscious.

A little explanation is okay and may even help. For instance, Mom may confess, "When you were born, Dad had just lost his job and I was obsessed with how we were going to survive. I wasn't able to bond with you as I wanted to." Or she says, "I was able to be home with [name of sibling] when he was little, but I needed to work when you were born. I would have loved to have been your full-time Mom." But you shouldn't use the explanation to deny responsibility for the hurt.

An apology from Mother to Louise (Favored) and Estelle (Disfavored) might sound like this:

> I now recognize I have hurt both of you. I loved you both, but I treated you differently. I spent more time with [showed more affection to, spent more money on, confided more in] Louise and demanded more of [was stricter with, was more critical of] Estelle. I failed to recognize and encourage Estelle's gifts. This created false expectations in Louise and robbed her of a sister's love. It made Estelle feel less loved or worthy. It created jealousy between you. I was wrong. I am so very sorry. Please forgive me.

The disfavored brother can apologize to his parent for the pain he caused by acting out to get attention (or whatever else he may have done) and beating up on his little brother. He can apologize to his brother for that—for blaming him unfairly and for continuing to assume the worst.

The favored sister can apologize for lording it over the other one and taking advantage of her special status with Daddy—or for not developing a closer friendship with her sister.

If you take an inner "searching moral inventory" (as they say in AA), then you'll discover what to say.

Forgiveness

Once a heartfelt apology has occurred, forgiveness may be instant. The recipient may simply say, "Mom, I forgive you." Or, if a person needs time to work with it more, they can simply say, "Thank you for saying that. It couldn't have been easy." Or forgiveness may come in the form of an answering apology as illustrated above.

An apology helps the offended person to forgive in two ways: receiving and giving. Receiving an apology is healing. The desire for relationship is built into our genes. A rupture with a close family member carries deep pain. We long for reconciliation, and when it is offered with a sincere apology, most of us gladly receive it. The offender is suffering from the rupture as much as we are. Forgiveness is a natural response.

Second, when we apologize it also helps us forgive the offender. If we can recognize some fault on our own part, then we become less judgmental of our brother. This can be true even if the other person does not seek our forgiveness. Broken relationships are rarely one-way trips. Did you make a negative assumption instead of asking a question? Were you overly sensitive? Did you misunderstand the other's intention? Searching your own conscience may help you to forgive, even without a conversation about it.

Conversely, a "demand" for apology makes it almost impossible for the offender to apologize, even when they want to. As a mediator, Carolyn was once fifteen minutes late for a court appearance. She had rehearsed all the way into the courtroom the *mea culpa* she would offer. But before she could open her mouth, the judge started to berate her, with pointed finger, about how irresponsible she was. (Carolyn wondered how he would feel if he knew she was a retired judge, but she did not mention it!) She stood there mutely and took it, but she did not offer the apology she had rehearsed. Feeling humiliated, she clung to her last shred of dignity through silence. She really was sorry, but she was not going to grovel!

In retrospect, what should Carolyn have done? She wishes she had remembered that *a demand for an apology is really a disguised plea*. The offended person is saying, "Please help me forgive you. Make it easier." She should have just said, "I'm sorry I was late, Your Honor, and I'll try not to do it again."

In a mediation, after the parties have had a chance to talk about how they've been injured, we sometimes say something like, "You've each had an opportunity to talk about how you've been hurt by this dispute. Looking back now, is there anything you wish you'd done differently?" This often opens up an avenue for apology that was not available before.

What if I humble myself and apologize sincerely, but the other person won't forgive me?

That can happen. It hurts. But the one who apologized has done what they could do and, in fact, ought to have done. They can move on with a clear conscience—and, one hopes, with a spacious willingness to receive the other's forgiveness if and whenever it may come.

Suppose the other person never apologizes. Should I still forgive?

Yes. Forgiveness is not only a gift for another; it's a gift you give yourself. Forgiving the unapologetic does not mean you deny, condone, or minimize the hurt another has caused you. It doesn't mean forgetting. It doesn't require you to continue to live with someone who mistreats you. It doesn't mean surrendering the need for accountability. It means opting for freedom.

Carrying a grudge can become very heavy. Freedom lies in letting it go. A friend once said this about forgiving her unrepentant ex-husband, who had abandoned her with four children for a younger woman: "One day I just got tired of giving him free rent in my head. I can't tell you how good it felt to kick him out."

In the novel *Crooked Little Heart*, Anne Lamott writes that "holding onto a resentment is like eating rat poison and waiting for the rat to die."[4] A helpful book for someone struggling with forgiveness issues is *The Book of Forgiving: The Fourfold Path for Healing Ourselves and Our World* by Desmond Tutu and Mpho Andrea Tutu.

Try this: Picture your enemy as a wounded child. What may be the source of his pain? Or write a letter to the one who has harmed you. Say exactly what you think and feel. Spare nothing. Then burn it. Cast the ashes to the wind. And let it go.

Worst Case Scenarios: Court Fights

Unforgiven sibling wounds often end up in court, especially near or after the death of a parent. They are ugly. And can get very, very expensive.

A Grandmother's Power of Attorney

In one case, a grandmother had appointed one of her five grandchildren as her financial agent under her general power of attorney (POA). Even though this grandchild lived some distance from her grandmother, they enjoyed an emotionally warm and caring relationship. After several years, two of the other grandchildren decided to contest the granddaughter's POA authority. They alleged that the grandmother's mental capacity was failing and that the POA holder was not taking sufficient measures to protect their grandmother's safety. Although the grandmother admittedly was unable to maintain her financial records, she was alert and aware of everything going on around her. And she did not want to modify her granddaughter's role.

What followed was unfortunate: the allegedly aggrieved grandchildren pursued their case in court. After two years of expensive and emotionally exhausting litigation (especially for the aging grandmother), they were able to mediate a mutually acceptable outcome. But guess who footed the legal expenses? That's right: the grandmother who never wanted the case to go forward in the

---

4. Anne Lamott, *Crooked Little Heart* (New York: Anchor, 1998).

first place wound up paying tens of thousands of dollars to everyone's attorneys.

A lot of tough conversations could be made easier if we could (1) value the autonomy of older adults and (2) drop our expectations that others can't (or won't) meet.

On the Trail of the DNA

As we mentioned earlier in this chapter, Carolyn was assigned a court case involving an exhumed body. (Identifying details have been changed, but the story is true!)

The deceased father had tried to make a will, leaving his estate (approximately $500,000) equally to his five named children. But the will was declared void for a technicality. No problem. The rules of intestacy should have produced the same result: five children, equal division. Each would get about $100,000. Simple, right?

One brother won the race to the courthouse and was named personal representative. Instead of promptly dividing the estate, he hired his son as the estate's lawyer and began to pay him a fee. The brother also took one for himself as administrator. He made no distributions to his siblings. The other siblings had to file suit to try to get this brother and his son removed. In addition to defending himself (legal expenses paid from estate funds—to his son—while the plaintiffs had to hire and pay their own lawyer), he alleged that one child, living abroad, was not the father's biological daughter (although this daughter had been named in the original will and she produced a Vietnamese birth certificate naming the father). The other four children had not been raised with her, but they had heard about her and agreed that she was their half-sister.

After the fifth appearance in court, the judge ordered the father exhumed (at the estate's expense). The DNA matched. By then the estate was reduced to $50,000. Each sibling (except the personal representative and his son, who had already collected the lion's share in fees) received $10,000 instead of $100,000 of their father's intended legacy.

"The Good Daughter"

Tammy Darvish was the daughter of John Darvish Sr., a prominent car dealer in the Washington, DC, area.[5] When she learned she was being passed over for leadership in the family-owned company, Tammy sued her father (whom she adored) and two stepbrothers, claiming that their father had promised her that his children would run the company together when he retired. The judge expressed sympathy for Tammy and acknowledged her faithful years of service and her expectation of being rewarded. But in the absence of a written agreement, she was unable to prove the father's promise. The case was dismissed.[6] The family was destroyed.

Two Sisters: A Happy Ending

Cecily and Margot are sisters whose relationship has been loving but prickly. Feelings are easily wounded, so both try to tread carefully. Margot has a grown daughter; Cecily's son Thomas, about the same age, took his own life five years ago.

Time has passed, but Cecily's grief has not. She and her husband decided to mark Thomas's passing with a "celebration" to try to emphasize their late son's gifts of music and art and their enduring love for him. They invited their large extended family to attend.

Margot's daughter shocked Cecily with a cruel and unfair e-mail response to the invitation. "You are a violent person," she wrote. "No wonder Thomas killed himself. You killed him. I will not attend your phony display of grief." And it went on. The niece copied her mother on the e-mail.

Cecily was floored. But instead of reacting instantly—by responding angrily to her niece, or sharing the e-mail with all the family members to show how awful her niece was, or attacking Margot for raising such a child, or emphasizing her own suffering—she paused. A week passed, and when she had not heard from

---

5. Roxanne Roberts, "The Good Daughter," *The Washington Post*, April 2, 2015.

6. Roxanne Roberts, "The End of the Darcars Family Drama?," *The Washington Post*, June 8, 2016.

Margot, Cecily consulted her husband and a trusted friend about how to respond.

The friend advised, "Margot should reach out to you, but she may feel ashamed or embarrassed or afraid to say the wrong thing. Why don't you let her know you need her?"

So instead of waiting and insisting that Margot make the first move, Cecily did. She acknowledged that Margot's daughter is an adult and responsible for her own remarks, so she wasn't blaming Margot. She also said she recognized that her niece has had some psychological problems. But, she said, the e-mail was very, very hurtful. Cecily said she found it incomprehensible that her niece could write such a thing. She repeated that the loss of Thomas was immensely tragic and painful, it is with her every day, and it will continue to be until she dies. Then she took the risk of making a request: "I need you to contact me about this. The warm support of family and friends can help with this reality."

Margot's response was both thoughtful and healing. She understood Cecily's reaction, she said, but she asked her to look beneath her daughter's words to her own suffering and her framework for seeing the world. Margot confessed that she and her husband are the targets of similar attacks; that the slightest request sets their daughter off.

Then Margot made her own request: "So, Cecily, please don't take her e-mail at face value, but rather as the confessions of a wounded heart and a distraught soul." She closed with a kiss.

Both sisters did the right thing. Because their relationship could be fragile, they stuck to e-mail rather than risk a person-to-person or telephone exchange. (This might not be best under other circumstances. Harsh things that are written, such as the niece's message, can take on a life of their own.) They paused, thought about possible responses, consulted with others they could trust to keep a confidence, tried to put themselves in one another's place, described their own feelings, and made a request.

This exchange left both sisters feeling closer than ever before. It was healing for Cecily. And it even opened the door for her to understand and forgive the niece, whether or not that niece may ever be able to apologize.

A Personal Note from Carolyn on Blended Families

Second marriages are as common as clover and generally encouraged by society (over eternal singleness). Marriage brings companionship, optimism, improved nutrition and health, increased longevity, and often financial stability. And second mates are likely to become caregivers when sickness strikes, relieving adult kids of that responsibility.

But after a certain age, adult kids may find it hard to accept another person in their parent's life. They may still be grieving the loss of their missing parent, even though time has passed and the parent may have died. Their first response may be, "Mom can't be serious! She's just lonely and likes the idea of having someone to take her to the movies once in a while. It's okay." Or, "We don't want you to be lonely, Dad. We want you to be happy. Really. Just so it doesn't get serious." Then: "Well, it's okay if you move in together, but you're not thinking of marriage, are you? *Are you?* Really?!"

If sibling rivalry presents issues as parents age, then stepsiblings and parents you didn't grow up with take it to another level. Will a stranger get Mom's jewelry? Dad's memorabilia? What about their investments? Will Mom or Dad change their will? Powers of attorney? We thought we knew what we were likely to inherit, and now all bets are off!

My story: My husband Jerry died in 2015. After fifty-six years of marriage I never expected to marry again. Nevertheless, two years later I did. Jim, one of Jerry's best friends and a former Secret Service colleague, had also lost a spouse after a long marriage. We'd known each other (as couples) for at least forty years. We were both lonely. We had similar values. We liked and trusted each other. We found each other attractive and discovered we enjoyed each other's company. We fell in love, and in 2017 we married.

Jim has four adult children and I have three, all around the same ages. We wanted their approval, and we wanted to reassure them they would benefit, not lose out, from our union. Here's what we did.

Before we married we tried to make it easy for our kids to know each other. For instance, I gave a birthday party for Jim at my then-home and invited all children and grandchildren from both sides. They mingled well. We got acquainted with each other's children, and they with each other. One child from each side was absent, so a few months later my daughter Jennifer gave a party at her house and invited everyone again. She and two of Jim's kids lived in Severna Park, Maryland, near Annapolis (where Jim also lived), but they previously didn't know each other. Jennifer and Jim's daughter Michele hit it off and made plans to get together again.

We involved the kids in helping us find a new home. Jim and I decided to buy a place together rather than move into one of our current homes. We chose Annapolis because (1) it was close to Severna Park and our kids if a crisis struck; (2) it had more amenities than Severna Park, such as public transportation, nice restaurants and shopping centers, the Naval Academy, and St. John's College; (3) it had less traffic and congestion and fresher air than Washington, DC, where I lived; and (4) I'd grown up near water and hoped for a condo with a view of the Chesapeake Bay or one of its tributaries. Michele and Jennifer researched places for us, made good suggestions about offering a contract, and Michele and Marco, Jim's youngest son, accompanied us and our realtor to look at places we liked. They also helped us negotiate a fair price for the one we settled on. Their recommendations were very helpful.

We wrote a prenuptial agreement and shared it with all the children. The purpose of a prenuptial agreement (prenup) is to determine, before marriage, how the property each brings to the marriage will be distributed in the event of death or divorce. We wanted the kids to know that our marriage would not take away anything they would have inherited had we not married.

Our lawyer said we needed to do two things in the prenup: first, write out in an appendix our individual assets that would *not* be considered "marital property," and second, waive our right to take a "statutory share" of each other's will.[7] The prenup can provide for

---

7. Every state provides that a spouse cannot be disinherited and is entitled by law to a prescribed share of their deceased mate's estate, whether named in the will or not, or even if there is no will. In Maryland, the share is one-third if the deceased left children. This right can be waived.

other things as well, such as inheritances or gifts we might receive from others after the marriage. Anything not specifically carved out is marital property, to be shared as the prenup, our wills, or state law provides.

In the interest of transparency, we showed our kids the draft of our prenup. We tried to answer their questions, and then made some changes. Although we didn't adopt all their suggestions, we did try to respond to their concerns.

Finally, we invited all the children to help plan our wedding, participate with readings or toasts, and to stand up with us as our attendants. Even a British Royal Family wedding probably had fewer attendants—we had ten on each side—but we and our guests loved it!

We're so grateful for each other and for all the children, including the other's. We hope we've headed off any conflicts among the step-siblings that might arise upon our deaths. Wherever we go, when strangers hear that we're newlyweds (at our age!) they break into smiles. It makes them happy. I think we're a symbol of hope.

What Can Happen Instead of Hostility

There are plenty of families where siblings collaborate, divide the duties of handling finances, organizing caregiving, driving an older parent to doctors' appointments or social events, or just keeping the parents company. In these cases flexibility, transparency, and openness characterize a healthy interplay among the siblings. In family conferences involving an elderly parent, brothers and sisters can acknowledge, "We do have some old, angry feelings toward each other. But we all love Mom and want the best for her. Our love for her is greater than our hurt with each other. We *can* work together on this."

The same "truths" apply to all healthy relationships: between friends, siblings, and generations. Here they are:

- *Forgiveness.* Don't keep score. Know a mountain from a molehill—and think of the little stuff as endearing instead of letting it drive you nuts. And try not to go to bed mad.

- *Attention.* For at least an hour a day, stop multitasking, turn off the screens, and listen to each other.

- *Generosity.* Live out of an image of plenty, not scarcity. Help others, be hospitable, and give your money, time, and energy to improve the world.

- *Support.* Be each other's biggest fans. Have each other's backs. Make each other laugh. Mourn each other's losses. Celebrate each other's triumphs.

- *Shared Spirituality.* Rabbi Jonathan Sacks says, "God is bigger than religion." By shared spirituality, we mean creating safe space to share one's spiritual understandings—about God, about the meaning of life, about the deepest things you each believe.

- *Gratitude.* Give thanks every day for three or more blessings you enjoy, even if things are challenging. It helps you remember the gift that you are to one another.

You and those you love will have different experiences and search for different truths. But together you can discover a common well from which you all may drink, one that can sustain you as a family over the long haul.

6

SCALING THE TWIN PEAKS OF PAPERWORK AND PLANNING

BY CAROLYN AND SIG

Part 1: The Documents

It was nearly midnight, but Charlie's outdoor cats would not stop howling. Exasperated, a neighbor knocked on Charlie's door to remind him to fill their water and food bowls. When he received no answer he became alarmed. By the time police found Charlie's body, he had been dead several days.

A Miami detective called Carolyn's husband Jerry to tell him. Jerry and Charlie were army buddies from way back. Charlie had no wife, no kids, no siblings. He'd left a note with Jerry's number. Charlie wanted Jerry to have his house and everything in it.

Charlie thought he'd arranged everything. Jerry was the designated payee on Charlie's bank account. Jerry was co-owner of Charlie's safe deposit box. Jerry was named as personal representative and residuary legatee in an unsigned copy of the will Charlie's lawyer had sent. What could possibly go wrong?

Plenty.

For starters, the "will" was a copy, not a signed and witnessed original. Neighbors said they saw Charlie sign it, and they signed it as witnesses. But it couldn't be found. It was not in any obvious place in Charlie's house or car, and the lawyer had not kept the original.

Then there was this: Charlie was a hoarder. Loose, unmarked papers were piled high in every room of the three-bedroom house, including the kitchen and a bathtub. Nearly $3,000 in cash and undeposited checks was stuffed under sofa cushions and inside the pockets of his jeans. Unread magazines buried unpaid water and electric bills. Lapsed insurance policies, overdue property tax bills, and mortgage reminders threatening repossession nestled among underwear in a chest of drawers.

Jerry immediately hired a local lawyer who obtained a court order to go into Charlie's lock box to look for the will. (He'd never told Jerry he was the co-owner so Jerry thought he needed a court order.) It wasn't there. A month passed. Still nothing. Meanwhile, although the will's copy described how Charlie wanted to be buried, the coroner was loath to release the body to Jerry, who was not a blood relative. The coroner eventually gave in, and Charlie was cremated as he wished, but only after a three-week struggle (and daily charges for refrigerating the body).

Five weeks after Charlie died, the court-ordered executor found the signed will in a file labeled "Veterinarian" under a four-foot stack of quilts.

It's not uncommon for an older adult to believe their planning is done if they have made a will. But one has to tell the named primary legatee or personal representative *where* to find all important papers! And the will is just the beginning.

Legal Documents Everyone Needs

Every adult, regardless of age, needs three legal documents: A testamentary plan (will or trust or both), a durable power of attorney (for financial and legal matters), and an advance directive for health care (in two parts, a health-care power of attorney and a living will). These are sometimes called by other names, which we'll get to below.

A Testamentary Plan (Will and/or Trust)

This is a written declaration of how you want to dispose of your property after death. A will can be changed at any time prior to the maker's death or incapacity.[1]

---

1. "Incapacity" is a flexible term. A person may not be able to continue handling their own financial affairs, but they may be clear on whom they want

A testamentary plan may also include trusts,[2] life insurance, pensions, and titling property to provide a survivor or beneficiary. Some of these arrangements allow a beneficiary to escape probate[3] and simply produce a death certificate in order to collect the asset. Be aware that avoiding probate is not the same as avoiding taxes. Some arrangements are taxable and some are not. A local lawyer familiar with estate planning and probate should draw up the will.

Here's what happened with Jerry and Charlie.

Charlie had named Jerry as his executor[4] as well as residuary legatee (the person who would receive everything left after bills were paid and specific gifts were distributed). Since Jerry's wife (Carolyn) was a retired lawyer, Charlie made her the alternate executor. The lawyer who drew up the will was Charlie's neighbor, specializing in landlord-tenant matters.

When Charlie died, a new lawyer realized that neither Jerry nor Carolyn could serve as executor, because in Florida the personal representative had to be a spouse, a blood relative, or a Florida resident. That ruled out both of Charlie's choices. Although Carolyn is an active member of the bars of Maryland and the District of Columbia, as well as the U.S. Supreme Court, she did not qualify in Florida. Charlie's neighbor-lawyer did not know that. Jerry had to hire a Florida probate lawyer and incur extra expense to appoint a qualified executor/resident.

We are constantly stunned (if not flabbergasted) by the number of notables who don't have a will. Supreme Court Chief Justice

---

to handle them. If they understand what a will is and who they want to receive their possessions, they probably have capacity to sign a will or POA, even if they have been diagnosed with early dementia.

2. People may use trusts for a number of reasons, including avoidance of probate. (A trust will not avoid estate taxes, however.) Trusts can be complex and are too big a topic to tackle here. You should contact an attorney specializing in estate matters for legal advice.

3. "Probate" is a legal process that involves an heir or executor proving to a judge that the deceased's will is valid, paying outstanding debts and taxes, and distributing the property.

4. An "executor" is the person named in the will to carry out its terms. If there is no will, an "administrator" is appointed by the court to distribute property according to state law. The generic term for both is "personal representative."

Warren Burger died intestate. So did James Gandolfini (who played Tony Soprano in *The Sopranos*). And Aretha Franklin. And Prince. Can you imagine the amount of energy, money, and time that will go into dividing their estates? In her recent column in *The Washington Post*, financial expert and commentator Michelle Singletary reported that a 2017 Gallup Poll found that only 44 percent of the respondents had a will. Worse, this percentage had declined from the 51 percent Gallup surveyed in 2005. Reader, do *you* have one?[5]

Durable Power of Attorney (POA)

This document contains instructions *in writing* in which the principal (perhaps a parent) grants another person (perhaps an adult child) authority to act as their "agent" to perform certain specified acts on their behalf. A POA can be for a specific purpose, such as transferring out-of-town property, which would expire when the purpose is served or the maker becomes incapacitated. In contrast, a *durable* POA survives the principal's incapacity. A durable POA is sometimes referred to as a "Financial Power of Attorney," because the individual named is authorized to make financial decisions on behalf of the principal on such matters as check signing, modifying the principal's assets, or disposing of property. It gives the agent power to sign the principal's name as if signed by the principal. It is indeed a powerful instrument and should never be given to anyone whose judgment you do not trust completely.

We recently learned of such an instance. A nephew (named George) wanted his Uncle Milt (for whom he held power of attorney and was his only living relative) to move to a nursing home near his residence in another state. Milt resisted. After months of

---

5. Michelle Singletary, "I Wasn't Surprised That Aretha Franklin Didn't Have a Will: You Probably Don't, Either," *The Washington Post*, August 23, 2018, G-3. When Sig's mother passed away, she left neither a will nor a trust. Since all her assets were either in her bank or her brokerage account, she executed a Transfer on Death (TOD) document. The TOD automatically transferred everything to Sig and his sister as beneficiaries and, in this case, in equal amounts. All they had to do was produce a death certificate for the transfers to be executed. No probate. No fees. Simple. If you decide on this option, be sure to check whether your state has any special regulations relating to TODs.

trying to get Milt's permission, George used his role as agent in his uncle's POA to forcibly take Milt to the nursing home. We cannot imagine how traumatic this must have been for Milt, who had been living independently and had a good support system.

What can you do to prevent such an occurrence?

1. Remember that the power given to your agent to sign on your behalf is legally binding. So, get his or her agreement upfront to follow your wishes. If you sense any pushback, choose another agent.

2. To protect yourself from premature use, don't give your signed and witnessed POA to your agent right away. Keep it in a safe place and tell the agent (or someone you trust) where it is, but withhold immediate access.

3. Add some limiting language, such as "This document shall become effective upon the written determination of two doctors that I am not capable of making informed decisions about [my own health care] or [my finances]."

4. You can also revoke a power of attorney by writing a simple revocation or creating a new document naming a new agent with language that revokes all prior POAs. It must be in writing and witnessed. Send copies to everyone who might have received the first one.

Advance Directive

An advance directive applies to health and medical matters. It normally contains two elements:

1. A health-care (or medical) power of attorney names someone whom the maker trusts to talk to their doctors and receive medical information, as well as to make critical health-care decisions for them if they are unable to speak on their own behalf.[6]

2. A living will specifies the kinds of medical treatment a person may or may not want when they can no longer make decisions

---

6. According to the Mayo Clinic website, a person designated to make these decisions may be called one of the following: health-care agent, health-care proxy, health-care surrogate, health-care representative, or health-care attorney-in-fact.

for themselves. It helps guide family members and medical professionals (though it may not be legally binding on the doctor).

Unlike a will, an advance directive doesn't need to be prepared by a lawyer to be effective. Hospitals and nursing homes often provide forms, and many states have them as well. For instance, one state form is headed "Maryland Advance Directive: Planning for Future Health Care Decisions."[7] It comes in two parts, with simple blanks to fill in. Part I is "Selection of Health Care Agent" (otherwise known as a Medical Power of Attorney"). Part II is headed "Treatment Preferences ('Living Will')." A person can fill out either or both sections, sign, and have it witnessed by two people who will not inherit from them or be named in the document. (In Washington, DC, medical employees associated with the grantor's care are also precluded as witnesses.) In Maryland, a notary public is not required, but it is in some states. Check your local rules.

Prenuptial Agreements

In the case of second marriages with blended families, many couples will also want to create a prenuptial agreement. You should consult a lawyer to be sure yours complies with your state law.

As previously mentioned, a prenup is a contract entered into *before marriage* (*pre*nuptial) between the future spouses. It lists the property each brings to the marriage and their wishes as to what will be excluded from the state's definition of "marital property" in case the marriage ends by death or divorce. It may have other provisions, such as excluding future inheritances or gifts. Furthermore, the prenup usually provides that each spouse waives the right to claim a "statutory spousal share" of the other's property at time of death. (Every state has laws providing that a spouse cannot be disinherited. The percentage of the estate is determined by statute but usually ranges from one-third to one-half.) One benefit of a prenup is to assure adult kids that the new spouse will not claim the inheritance the children are expecting. This waiver does not preclude spouses from leaving or giving gifts to each other.

---

7. This is available free from www.marylandattorneygeneral.gov.

Mistakes to Avoid

Many people confuse (or conflate) "financial powers of attorney" and "health-care powers of attorney." Don't. Do. That.

While both are enormously important legal documents, they call for different skill sets. If you are named as Dad's agent in a *durable power of attorney*, you should be familiar with his financial affairs, including income, taxes, property, and debt. You may have access to Dad's bank accounts,[8] a key to his safety deposit box (or at least know where it is and be listed with the bank), know the amount and location of his other assets, and understand mortgages and other debts, if any, Dad has incurred. You should be able to balance a checkbook and understand an ordinary tax return.

On the other hand, if Mom designates you as her *health-care agent*, at some point you may be required to choose a doctor, get a second opinion, and even make life or death decisions about whether to continue her on life support, undertake one or more major surgeries, or allow her to end her life peacefully at home or in hospice. You should know the names of Mom's doctors, have access to her medical record and prescriptions, and know her preferences for what some refer to as "heroic measures," such as feeding tubes, intensive care, and risky medical procedures from which she might survive or perish. *It's important that the person named does not have religious or other scruples against following the desires laid out in the living will.*

It also makes sense for Mom or Dad to designate one or more alternate agents in powers of attorney for both financial matters and health-care issues. It's possible the primary agent might predecease the parent or simply be unavailable or unwilling to serve in an emergency.

---

8. This can also be achieved by Dad's adding your name to the account *as an approved signer*. But he should *not* make you a *joint owner* of the account unless he intends to give you *all* the money when he passes. Sometimes parents change their account to a joint account for convenience, but they don't realize that joint account money will not pass through the will. Even if the parent intended it to be distributed to others or shared equally, it will all go to the joint owner.

Don't confuse an "advance directive" with a "Do Not Resuscitate" (DNR) order. Regardless of the patient's wishes, a DNR *must be signed by a physician in order to be binding on medical personnel.* A DNR only applies to cardiopulmonary resuscitation when an individual's heart stops and/or breathing fails. Some people mistakenly think it applies to the whole range of emergency measures, such as ventilation or artificial hydration. It doesn't.

If you call 911 and show the emergency medical team member your unconscious mother's living will that says she does not want to be resuscitated, *they will ignore you and do it anyway without a signed DNR from a doctor, on a state-approved form.* A DNR should be kept on the refrigerator where it can be easily spotted.

A "Physician's Order for Life Sustaining Treatment" (POLST; sometimes called MOLST, POST, MOST, or something similar) is another form a doctor must sign in order for it to take effect. It includes a DNR and also may state what treatments (surgery, antibiotics, intubation, and so on) are to be given or not given for a person nearing life's end.

Advance Care Planning

The advance directive described above should (but doesn't have to) result from a process called "Advance Care Planning." This is a *conversation* with one's doctor and family to clarify what medical treatments a patient would or would not want if they could no longer speak for themselves. Patients are encouraged to voice their values and what is most important to them as they consider the end of life. What does quality of life mean to them? How would they wish to be treated under certain circumstances? Where do they want to die? To be buried? Whom do they want as caregivers? Under what circumstances would they want simple pain relief (palliative care) rather than extraordinary measures to extend life?

One tangible end result of the conversation is a living will and the health-care power of attorney, the legal documents described above. But the conversation may also concern intangibles such as where a person wants to die, whom they hope will be with them, and their deepest fears about abandonment or becoming a burden to their children. Talking about these important matters can draw a family closer together.

It may take time (and patience) to initiate and engage your parents in "The Conversation," but it is worth every ounce of emotional and psychological energy you have.

Words vs. Deeds

According to the Conversation Project's website (www.conver sationproject.org), a 2012 survey of Californians found that 82 percent of the state's population feels it's important to put their wishes in writing, but only 23 percent have actually done it.[9] Another survey found that 90 percent of the population says that talking with loved ones about end-of-life care is important, but only 27 percent have actually done so.[10] And a Centers for Disease Control survey revealed that 60 percent of the population says that making sure their family is not burdened with tough decisions is "extremely important," but 56 percent of the population has not communicated their end-of-life wishes to family members.[11]

Five Wishes and Other Resources

One helpful tool that makes parent-child dialogue easier is Five Wishes (https://fivewishes.org), which is an example of an advance directive that challenges us to discuss its contents with family members before completing it. It is unique among other advance directives and living wills because it is user-friendly and easy to complete. It is available in twenty-eight languages, including Braille. Five Wishes meets the legal requirements for advance directives in forty-two states and the District of Columbia, and it has helped millions of people plan for and receive the kind of end-of-life care they want.

---

9. Survey of Californians by the California Health Care Foundation (2012). "Final Chapter: Californians' Attitudes and Experiences with Death and Dying," Lake Research Partners Coalition for Compassionate Care of California (February 2012), https://www.chcf.org/publication/final-chapter -californians-attitudes-and-experiences-with-death-and-dying/, 2.
10. The Conversation Project National Survey (2013).
11. Centers for Disease Control (2005).

Five Wishes began when Jim Towey, Mother Teresa's legal advisor, was working and living in her Washington, DC-based hospice. Mother Teresa's life and work became the inspirational basis for the document, which has been called "the living will with a heart and soul." The mission of its source, Aging with Dignity, is to affirm and safeguard the self-respect of individuals as they age and to promote better care for those near the end of life.

"Making Your Wishes Known" (www.makingyourwishesknown .com) is another excellent resource for those thinking about or ready to prepare their advance directive. The website caringly leads the user through the steps of preparing an advance directive and explains all the options one needs to know about end-of-life alternatives.

If your parents have signed an advance directive, *be sure to ask where they keep such documents.* Sig has sent each of his kids copies on a flash drive, plus they're in his wife's loose-leaf notebook (as discussed below).

Transparency with Family Members: Pros and Cons

Whether or not your parents share the contents of their wills is ultimately their decision. They may be completely open about distributing their assets, their intended donations to a favorite charity, or their debts. Or not.

We recommend as much transparency as parties are comfortable with, but transparency is a relative term. Whomever one chooses to act on one's behalf should be asked if they are willing to do so and told what is desired. Transparency can range from allowing the children to decide, for example, who will serve as a parent's health-care agent, financial agent, or executor of a will, to sharing documents before they are written and signed, to simply revealing them and offering to answer questions after they are signed. At a minimum, one should tell the children who the agents and executor are and where to find the documents when the parents die.

Parents may want to share some documents but not others. *Advance directives should always be shared, because everyone needs to understand the parents' last wishes.*

The degree of transparency may also depend not only on the parents' comfort but also on the closeness of a family and the level of trust in one another. Parents may want to keep things closer to the vest in high-conflict families. Problems such as addiction, spendthrift activity, a child's shaky marriage, controlling in-laws with an agenda, or a family secret (such as a child born out of wedlock) may also weigh against complete transparency.

Special sensitivity is required when a parent marries a second spouse late in life (see chapter 5). For purely practical reasons, such as probable proximity when one falls ill, the couple may want to change their health-care agent from a child previously named to their new spouse. They may also want to change their financial agent and executor, but these may be less crucial. It's a good idea to have those duties, especially that of executor, filled by a younger person who is likely to survive the decedent.

If an adult child has been replaced, they may feel pushed out of their parent's affection, no matter how loving and trustworthy the step-parent may be. The child may also still be grieving the lost parent, even if a number of years have passed. Regardless of their age, children need to be reassured that love is not a zero-sum game. They are as loved and important to the parent as before. The creation and sharing of a prenuptial agreement (as discussed above) should go a long way toward building trust.

Ordinarily, greater transparency will prevent misunderstandings among heirs caused by surprises or disappointments when the will is read. Prior revelation will open a channel for discussion about reasons for parental decisions.

Should You Designate Gifts by Need or Equality?

If parents want to give to children according to need rather than equally, this probably should be revealed and explained. Amelia, for example, is a talented but struggling artist, while her sister Margarita is a well-established brain surgeon. The parents want to encourage Amelia by leaving her more money so she can be under less stress in trying to develop her art into a paying profession. In this case, Mom and Dad really should have a conversation with

Margarita first (who may readily agree), and then with Amelia. But if parents remain silent, Margarita may wonder whether they loved her less. She may also turn on Amelia, believing she influenced the parent's decision to give her the most. So it's usually best to give kids a heads-up.

But parents may have other reasons not to disclose their finances. Wealthy parents may fear that disclosure will provoke greed or act as a disincentive for their children to work. (Gloria Vanderbilt left nothing to her son, CNN newscaster Anderson Cooper, for that reason. He was okay with that.) Parents who have little may not want to worry their children about their own need—or they may be ashamed of an IRS lien on their home or other debt. Other parents may not want the children to begin to think of the parents' money as their own.

Whatever a parent's tolerance for transparency, they should *at least* tell their children *whether or not* they have a will and, if so, (1) where the signed and witnessed original (which must be filed for probate) is kept, and (2) the name of the executor. Lack of this information can result in prolonged court procedures and delayed distribution of assets. And if the will can't be found, the court will treat the decedent as having died *intestate* and determine distribution by state intestacy statutes. Even if all heirs agree on what the parents wanted, a court will not consider such evidence.

Regarding transparency, if your parents divulge some or all of their will's provisions to you, please encourage them to do the same with your siblings. Imagine how you'd feel if after your parents' deaths you learn that a sister or brother knew of their bequests and you were in the dark. Or even that one of them had a hand in preparing the wills. Trust between you and your siblings could be weakened, perhaps permanently.

As the Farmers' Insurance guy says: "We've seen it all!"

Sharing Other Information

Having the right documents and telling the family is not all that's required. As Jerry learned from his buddy Charlie, sharing other information is also crucial.

Sig's friend Georgine was completely unprepared when her husband recently passed away. While he had plenty of life insurance and a generous pension, he failed to inform his wife about his bank and brokerage accounts, record passwords to his bank accounts, retirement plan, and other important Internet-based financial sites, or write down the combination to a safe in their home. (He also failed to divest himself of thirty-two cameras, forty-two suits, and baskets of coaxial, telephone, and electrical wire, but that's another story.)

Georgine's memories of her late husband are loving. But before she could grieve her loss, she had to tend to myriad details concerning her financial well-being. Inexplicably, her bank shut down two joint checking accounts she shared with her late husband. A month after his funeral, she still couldn't access these accounts. And the bank refused to autopay her bills, such as utilities and mortgage.

Georgine needed a Need-to-Know Notebook.

Putting It All Together

Last year—like every year for that matter—I (Sig) wrestled with what to get my wife for her birthday. Dismissing flowers, dinner out, or a Whitman's Sampler of chocolates, I pondered what to give her.

At various times my wife has asked me: "What am I supposed to do in an emergency?" "What if you get very sick, or worse, whom do I call?" "Where do I look for your insurance papers, information on your pension, and other things?"

When I showed her the file cabinet where I keep our vital documents, she protested: "How can anyone find anything in there?" So, I bought a loose-leaf notebook with plenty of tabs and set to work.

The first page lists only critical phone numbers: Whom to call regarding my pension if I pre-decease her, our retirement accounts, insurance companies, long-term care provider, and so on. Next came a table of contents. Then the tabs with the following content:

Tab A: An article from an investment magazine titled "Checklist for Surviving Spouses" and then a detailed list of our bank accounts, retirement plans with account numbers, and so on.

Tab B: Front page from our insurance policies and long-term care plans.

Tab C: Copy of my will.

Tab D: A spreadsheet listing the passwords and PIN numbers for websites for our bank, insurance company, phone and cable companies, and so on. That tab also has pages where I scanned the fronts and backs of our credit cards, driver's licenses, Medicare ID, and other information I carry in my wallet. Another page contains the front and back of our passports.

Tab E: Copies of our advance medical directives and powers of attorney for health-care and financial matters. (And information regarding where the originals are kept.)

Tab F: Descriptions of our respective funeral arrangements.

What I thought would take days to compile took only a *few hours*. There may be items I didn't think of. When I recall them, I'll pop them in the notebook. My wife reviewed it, thanked me for putting everything in *one* binder, and stored it where *she* can easily access it.

Missing or Outdated Documents

Celeste had a living will but no health-care power of attorney. When she suffered a stroke and was rushed to the hospital, one of her adult children gave a copy of the living will to the attending physician. It called for no extreme measures if it was evident Celeste would not survive an illness. All but one of her children agreed with that request. But the dissenter caused extreme distress to the whole family by insisting Celeste be put on a ventilator. Somehow Celeste had never included that child in her discussions with the others about how she wished to die. And she had no POA. There in the ER, the children had to vote on whether to let their mother die peacefully.

Another story: Dmitri was admitted to his local hospital with a severe heart condition. Though Dmitri had an advance directive, the doctors thought it didn't cover every possibility. If Dmitri lost consciousness and got worse, they might need a person to make decisions. "Did you designate an agent in a health-care power of attorney?" they asked.

Heavily sedated, Dmitri whispered, "Yes."

"Who?" his doctor asked. Dmitri named a former neighbor, Jack, who had moved to a different city ten years earlier. When the doctor finally tracked him down, Jack could barely remember Dmitri or recall how long ago they were neighbors. Jack refused to take responsibility.

Part 2: Preparing Your Family's Plan Together

To plan for the future, it's best to call a family conference. But that may be harder than it sounds. Who will take the initiative? Ordinarily, a parent should be the convener, but they may not want to talk about their own end of life. An adult child's reluctance to broach the topic of a parent's coming demise or incapacity is also common and understandable. You don't want to look greedy. You don't want your parents to think you're looking forward to their death or expecting it any time soon. (In fact, the thought of it may leave you in a state of panic.) So it's probably easier if your parent initiates the conversation. But if they hesitate, here are some tips to help kids get a discussion started:

- Focus on your own need for peace of mind, wanting to know their wishes so you can carry them out.

- You might mention a neighbor or relative's death and how their kids handled things.

- You might reveal that you have made (or are thinking about making) your own will and you want to share information with them. Or get their advice.

If parents are convinced that sharing information will help you, they're more likely to do it. If parents won't disclose basic information, then the siblings with knowledge (perhaps those living closest) can help create an atmosphere of transparency. That child might agree to:

- Update the other siblings every three or six months about their parents' health
- Inform them of any amendments in their parents' wills
- Share with them any major changes in financial affairs (with the parent's consent)
- Set up family phone conferences to update others on any changes

Divisions can be minimized if decisions are made openly and early enough to dispel jealousy and suspicion, and avoid surprises.

What Parents and Kids Want One Another to Know

To explore ways to start a conversation, we conducted a workshop where we invited parents and their adult kids to attend together. Fifty people participated, split about equally between parents and their adult children. After a joint session we separated them into two groups by age. The purpose was to help them discover topics they wanted to address with each other but hesitated to mention and to give them some tools to overcome their discomfort. We asked each group questions such as:

- What is your greatest concern about [your parents'] aging?
- How do you feel about discussing your [or their] health and finances?
- Where do you [or your parents] expect to live later in your life?
- What's your deepest hope for your [or your parents'] future?

Some of the participants' responses were expected; others were unexpected. Most of the seniors worried most about dependency, helplessness, and a consequential loss of freedom. They resisted role reversal. Some mentioned fear of abandonment.

But their kids almost unanimously said that parental driving was their biggest worry!

When asked what they want their children to know but are too reluctant to mention, some parents said finances. Others wondered how to tell kids they planned to leave unequal amounts to their children. Some children worried that a widowed parent might re-marry. These are tough issues to broach.

To our surprise, there was one question that older adults re-fused to even consider: *Do you want your children involved in your health-care decision-making and, if so, to what degree?* Each table of parents said they "ran out of time," but it was not the last question on the list (which they did manage to answer). We suspect that the question hinted at future helplessness, a topic that felt too dark.

When asked where they planned to live out their later years, predictably, most replied they wished to remain in their own homes. Some expressed a preference to live in an independent living resi-dence or continuing care community. But no one replied: *"With my children."* (Likewise, no children said they expected their parents to move in with them.)

Older adults' greatest hope for their future was that they keep their minds intact. One woman inspired us by saying, "If I do be-come helpless, I hope I can accept that with grace and find some meaning in it."

When the individual groups had shared their answers with the larger group, we said, "Now you can begin a conversation. On the way home, ask each other what happened in your group, and what did you contribute? How many think you can do that?" They all raised their hands.

Steps Families Can Take *Now*, Even without a Full-Blown Plan B

Compile a list of local senior resource providers such as senior centers, transportation services, grocery delivery, handyman ser-vices, grass cutting and snow shoveling, and house cleaning services.

Assemble names and contact information of parents' doctors, pharmacy, bank, attorney, accountant, and nearby hospital. If they belong to a faith organization, the name and phone of their pastor, priest, or rabbi.

Have a record of prescriptions and over-the-counter medicines that parents take. You'll need their Medicare number and any sec-ondary insurance plans.

Make sure powers of attorney (financial and health care) are up to date and family members have copies or know where to find them.

Making Plan B

To paraphrase Mike Tyson, everybody's got a plan until they get punched in the gut.

Your current situation is "Plan A." But, in addition to legal documents, everyone needs a "Plan B," planning for the unexpected (a broken hip, the onset of dementia, a fatal disease). Shockingly, few of us have a Plan B. A family may drift in a river of denial, oblivious to the waterfall around the bend. To get through the rapids, we'll need a map. But when should you make it?

Suppose Dad's recent physical exam reveals an enlarged prostate. Or Mom learns her vision is waning and she should stop driving at night. Or Grandma's declining memory impedes her capacity to spend money wisely. These are *issues*. They don't require immediate action, but they do signal that the time has come for a family sit-down to talk about Plan B.

An *emergency* occurs when Dad's urological functioning leads to chronic urinary tract infections and temporary hospitalizations. Or Mom has a fender-bender. Nothing serious, just some damage to both cars and traffic court for Mom. Or Grandma runs up $10,000 in credit card charges for items she buys on TV and forgets to open her purchases when they arrive. Emergencies are always precursors of *crises*.

A crisis comes when Dad is diagnosed with Stage 4 prostate cancer, and he can no longer live alone. Or Mom and the driver of another car are seriously injured in an accident where Mom was at fault. Or the IRS puts a lien on Grandma's condo.

When's the best time to make your plan? Whether you are at the issue phase, engulfed in an emergency, or confronting a crisis, *the time to begin is now*. There's no way to predict when a fatal accident, an incapacitating stroke, or another unexpected event will be your family's "Moment of Change"—the moment when what everyone hoped would never happen does happen. That's when lives are thrown, at least temporarily, upside down and panic trumps planning.

The good news is that thoughtful preparation can smooth the way through the darkness. Instead of everything coming apart, careful planning will bring the family closer together, whatever the challenge.

Other examples: A family's Plan A involves Dad caring for Mom who's in the early stages of memory loss. They live close to public transportation, church, a supermarket, bank, drug store, their doctors—in short, everything they need. The children live forty miles away. Everything seems to be working well.

But what if Dad is taken out of commission? A fall, an unforeseen medical emergency, even sudden death. Mom can't live alone. Is there a Plan B to respond to this "Moment of Change"?

If not, what might happen? An adult child has to take a leave of absence from their job to make emergency arrangements for Mom's care. In the rush to find suitable housing for an incapacitated parent, the adult child risks enrolling her parents into an inappropriate assisted living residence. The family is on a do-it-yourself track because no one researched local providers, such as senior centers, free or low cost transportation for handicapped persons, or geriatric support services.

Even when there is a will, it can be helpful to make a Plan B about a foreseeable disagreement that may arise after Mom's death. A shared vacation home is a common fire starter.

Jeanette and her family had spent every summer at the shore, and they all loved going there. Now the children had their own families, and Jeanette and the whole enlarged family still spent annual summer reunions together at the shore house.

When she contacted us, Jeanette was in the process of writing her will. She assumed the family would want to continue this tradition after she died. The thought of her future great-grandchildren playing in the waves made her smile. She planned to leave the shore house to her three children in equal shares. But there was a swarm of mosquitoes in this bucolic scene.

We advised her to call a family meeting to talk about it. Ten members, including in-laws and grandchildren, then met at Jeanette's house for supper and a conversation, and Carolyn moderated the discussion.

Everyone realized that the beach house is in a beautiful setting, an easy walk to the ocean and the small downtown area. It is large, old, and livable as is. But it needed a new roof, plumbing repairs, and a modernized kitchen—and, as one grandson pointed out, more comfortable furniture.

The first question Carolyn asked was, "Who is the decision-maker here?" After a little back and forth, all agreed that Jeanette had the last word. (Of course, she did legally, but it was good to clarify that point before the discussion began. The identity of the decision-maker should not be ambiguous. Jeanette wanted everyone's feedback, but ownership of her house would not be decided by a vote.)

As they went around the circle, many possibilities emerged, ranging from "bulldoze it and start over" (this from an in-law, who then conceded he would not push that view), to "make necessary repairs and continue using it as is," to "sell it and distribute the money so we can make other choices about vacations," to "spend $500,000 to upgrade it and make it a gorgeous, state-of-the-art place!" The children had widely varying incomes, and those with less wanted most to keep the house but could not afford a big contribution for repairs and upkeep. The child with the most income was willing to contribute more but didn't want to bear the entire financial burden.

Because this is an affectionate family, respectful and caring of their mother and one another, they reached agreement in this one session. Some ideas, like bulldozing or a $500,000 makeover, were voluntarily dropped. It was decided that Jeanette would pay for the new roof and plumbing now, and she would continue paying taxes and insurance until she passed. Also, she would create a trust fund for those expenses to be paid for three years after her death. A son offered to get estimates from local workers on the roof and plumbing. A daughter would get estimates and make suggestions about upgrading the kitchen, which everyone agreed was needed. A grandson would select new furniture, with an agreed dollar limit. Another son offered to be the point person for sharing all the incoming information with everyone by e-mail. All would report back to one another and Jeanette. As she approved of each step, work would begin.

This felt like a miracle to everyone present, and all were thoroughly on board. They had been heard, and accommodation to their wishes had been included as much as practically possible. Without the meeting (and good will), this could have been super ugly and may have ended up in court with family members choosing sides and not speaking to each other again. Nobody would have won. Instead, as far as the beach house was concerned, this family had created a very workable Plan B.

What's the best way to go about this if you decide to convene your own Plan B conference regarding your parents (or if you're the parent and want to hold this)? Here are some preliminary topics for discussion:

1. Who, if anyone, has access to your parents' healthcare, financial, and legal information? Where is it stored? We're not asking for the information here, only if someone knows where it's kept.

2. If the information resides in Dad's computer, ask him to back up the IDs and passwords, save them in a flash drive, and/or send copies to you and your siblings or another responsible person like his attorney. (And does Dad's attorney have your name and contact information?) If Dad is not tech savvy, offer to do it for him. Dad will have to remember to update this information whenever he changes a password.

3. Is there a safety deposit box? If so, what's in it? If anything happens to the owner of the box, who else is authorized—*and* has a key or knows where it is—to open the safety deposit box?

4. Do hard copies of your parents' information exist? If your parents don't live in your town, have they given you, a sibling, or their attorney instructions as to how to retrieve this information? Do you have copies of the front page of your parents' wills, trust documents, and insurance policies?

5. Ask your parents whether they have thought about where they want to live if they can no longer climb stairs or otherwise stay in their present home? (They may say, "We're staying here." If so,

let that be the answer for now. You can always revisit it later, if circumstances warrant.)

6. The hardest topic to broach may be final wishes. Have your parents chosen a church or funeral parlor where they would like to have last rites? If either parent served in the armed forces, would they like a military burial? Do they want to be cremated and have their ashes sprinkled in a special place? Or buried in a cemetery with close relatives? Have they made advance arrangements?

Wilson had shared all this information with his children, except for one item: his life insurance policies. After his unexpected death, it took weeks for his kids to comb through six file cabinets of papers to finally locate his insurance information. To avoid such a crisis, here's something for the children to add to their New Year's resolutions: *I will talk with my parents about how they assemble, collate, organize, and store all their financial and medical information that our family may need in case of their death.* And, regardless of your age, make sure your own spouse, offspring—whomever you deem essential—also have copies of your own data or access to where it's stored.[12]

Short of developing Plan B and building family member consensus around it, other short-term measures can help mitigate a crisis before it happens:

- Provide your parent with a "Life-Line" or other kind of wearable emergency alert system.
- Provide them with a cell phone.

This may take more than one conversation, but that's okay.

So, adult families, here's your homework: Get your testamentary plans (will or trust), financial powers of attorney, and advance directives (power of attorney for health care and living will) in order and talk about what's in them, and where they are stored. If you

---

12. Two organizations have made it easy for us to organize this information. Special thanks to the American Postal Workers Union and the Screen Actors Guild for their printable vital records organizers: http://www.apwu .org/dept/retiree/survivorsguide0909.pdf and http://www.sagph.org/html /vital.pdf.

don't already have one, make a Plan B (or even C) for unseen—but foreseeable—contingencies. Assemble and share information, including names of neighbors and doctors and the information below. Parents, talk to your adult kids. Children, talk to your parents—and to your own grown-up children.

Then sleep well. While you can't anticipate everything, you've done your best. Should caring for a parent or older loved one be in your stars, you're as well prepared as you can be.

7

CARING: GIVING AND RECEIVING

Part 1: The Gifts of Vulnerability

BY CAROLYN

"Here's how I want you to introduce yourself," Pastor Gordon Cosby began.

Eighteen adults of different ages, mostly strangers to each other, sat around a table on the third floor of Christ House, a hospital for homeless men in the Adams Morgan neighborhood of Washington, DC. We were students at the fledgling Servant Leadership School and had no idea what to expect.

"Don't tell us where you're from or what you do for a living," Gordon said. "We'll find that out soon enough. Just tell us your name and your deepest pain."

He waited calmly in the stunned silence.

Finally, a gray haired woman stood. "I know what my pain is, but I can't possibly tell it to a room full of strangers." She left.

A young, overweight woman spoke. "That's the most intimidating question I ever heard."

Gordon remained silent. She stayed.

Then an astonishing thing happened. Slowly, one by one, people began to speak. "My husband abandoned me and our four children for a younger woman. I can't forgive him."

A young man spoke, "I'm in my third year of seminary and have lost my faith."

My husband said, "My mother has Alzheimer's and no longer knows my name."

The pain kept flowing: "My sister just died of cancer. She was only twenty-seven years old."

"I have a broken relationship with my oldest daughter."

A woman crippled from childhood polio said, "I hate my leg."

Then the heavy young woman said, "I was bullied and teased as a child about my weight, and all my life I've felt ugly." She started to weep.

No one commented. No one offered to fix anyone else. Everyone just listened.

By the end of the two-hour session, it was clear that a miracle had happened: eighteen strangers had bonded. By going inward to discover and expose our deepest wounds, strangers had become a community. We were bound together, not by our strengths or credentials or social status. We were joined by mutual vulnerability.

The exercise taught me the value of self-awareness. And humility. And courage. And acceptance. And that, regardless of age, as human beings we are joined by compassion arising from shared pain.

As parents approach the last third of life, they experience more and more losses—physical, emotional, and mental. Their middle-aged children are not immune. In our fifties, we notice a few wrinkles and waffled thighs. Most of us no longer turn cartwheels. We get acquainted with bifocals. Our kids leave for college, and we have an empty nest. Our parents may begin to need us more and more.

In our sixties, we begin to turn up the volume on the television. We say "Pardon me?" more often. Then we retire and ask ourselves, "Who am I now?" In our seventies, we may have to stop driving. We're not as sharp as we once were, and some of us develop more serious memory loss.

Along the way, we begin to lose parents, friends, and sometimes spouses to illness and death. There may come a time when we're asked to care for them or our own spouse, or forced to receive care ourselves. The pain of the accumulating loss is real.

Here's the good news: aging is more than a process of loss. It also presents opportunities for development and growth, just like other life stages such as adolescence or young adulthood. In *How to Say It to Seniors*, David Solie notes that there are two principal developmental tasks for seniors: (1) creating a legacy that positively embeds us in the memories of our loved ones, and (2) learning to accept and live with our losses.[1] As long as we are alive, we have inner work to do. Surprisingly, our growing vulnerability—and that of those we love—can be the bearer of gifts.

The Gift of Compassion

My pastor said the best advice he ever got as a young minister was this: "As you look out into the congregation, remember that everyone you see is sitting with an invisible bucket of tears." When we're brave enough to peer into our own buckets, it becomes easier to imagine what others may be carrying.

In July 2014, I fell and broke my right ankle in three places. After emergency surgery (eight screws and a plate), I could not walk at all for six weeks or drive for three months. I was trapped. I felt totally helpless and, for the first time in my life, did not want to be alone for fear I would not be able to escape in an emergency. Others had to bring me food and water and help me to the bathroom.

One by-product of my own vulnerability was a deeper appreciation of the kindness of strangers—especially the immigrants of many hues and languages who bathed me gently, changed my bedpan without complaint, and worked cheerfully for a minimum wage doing the jobs nobody else wanted. One sang to me. If I invited their stories ("How did you come to America?" "Do you have a family here?"), I invariably heard tales of pain and struggle and hope. Their courage inspired me. How could I whine about a broken ankle that I knew would heal?

I also grew in compassion for people with handicaps. I'm ashamed to say I once resented an old person who held up a line in the supermarket while she struggled to coordinate a cane or walker and her purse. Now I think, *How brave she is to come grocery shopping alone! Good for her!*

---

1. David Solie, *How to Say It to Seniors* (New York: Prentice Hall Press, 2004).

The Gift of Gratitude

Paradoxically, acknowledging weakness can help us discover gratitude. Instead of asking "Why me?" I try to ask "What am I grateful for?"

A few years ago I began to keep a gratitude journal. I use a desk calendar from the Smithsonian's National Gallery of Art, because each page is lovely to look at and has enough room to write under each day of the week. Every morning, I write down something positive, even if yesterday was challenging. I try to name five blessings. There are days when I have to think hard to come up with even one.

Here's what I wrote on July 13, 2014—the day after I fell. With my leg wrapped in a splint and elevated, I could not move without help. Stuck. Hurting. The OxyContin that a nurse brought every twelve hours and the Dilaudid every four (my eye on large wall clock for the past thirty minutes) lowered the pain from an 8 (searing) to maybe 6.5 (throbbing) on a scale of 10. In desperation I reached for my gratitude journal. Here's what I wrote about the day before:

[I'm grateful for] kindness of strangers and acquaintances: Andy next door offered to walk and feed Spike. Elizabeth [the real estate agent who happened to be in my house when I fell] helped me get downstairs and offered to drive Jerry to the hospital behind the ambulance. Dr. D., the orthopedic surgeon, came in on a Sunday morning to operate. And Juan, our handyman and friend, drove in from Virginia on his day off to take Jerry home after I was admitted.

Okay, that was only four things. But I was happy for the drugs too! Although the care I was forced to receive came in a dark wrapper, it became a gift nonetheless.

The Gift of Courage

Brené Brown, an expert researcher on vulnerability, asked hundreds of people, "When was the last time you did something that you thought was really brave, or saw someone do something really brave?" Among the answers she received, *not one mentioned an experience that was not born of vulnerability.* She herself said, "The moments that made me who I am came from struggle."[2]

Courage is closely allied with risk, and risk involves making oneself vulnerable. The risk might be physical danger or rejection or the possibility of failure. When we're young, it takes courage to try to play a sport we may not be good at or to speak in public. When we leave home for college or fall in love, we feel the pangs of vulnerability—and the courage to move ahead in spite of it. We may choose an inherently dangerous career, such as law enforcement or military service. Nothing is more intimidating, however, than bringing that first baby home from the hospital!

Near life's end, courage takes on different forms. Bearing pain silently, and even accepting help with grace and gratitude, is brave. Caring for another adult is intimidating when we have no experience and may fail or make a mistake. I had to summon courage when I volunteered at The Gift of Peace AIDS hospice. I was intimidated, especially the first time I had to change a diaper on an adult. In old age, it takes courage to practice a foreign language or create art and show it to others. Confronting risk and moving ahead at any age—even if we might fail—is brave.

The Gift of Caring: A Sweet Burden

With a cotton ball dipped in hydrogen peroxide, Jerry gently swabbed the open sore on my father's bald head, and then he covered the sore with ointment. He did this every day. Dad was eaten up with prostate cancer that had metastasized everywhere and had recently popped out on top of his head. I overheard Dad say, his voice quivering, "I hate being a burden." Jerry paused, looked Dad in the eye, and said, "Art, if you're a burden, you're a sweet one." In truth, Jerry loved Dad as much as I did. And that love was returned.

Dad, however, was no longer the strong presence I grew up with and leaned on for support most of my life. I missed that fa-

---

2. Radio interview with Krista Tippet, "The Courage to Be Vulnerable," *On Being*, January 29, 2015.

ther. My father would never be the man he once was, but he rang the bells he could (as Leonard Cohen sang in "Anthem": "Ring the bells that still can ring"). As he grew weaker, he seemed to blossom emotionally. Previously, he was unable to say "I love you" (though he showed his love concretely and I never doubted it). Why? He grew up in a time when it didn't seem "manly" to express soft emotions. A man who did might be perceived as weak or vulnerable. But when he was in his nineties, Dad wrote in his journal, "I sure do love Carolyn and Jerry." He still could not bring the words to speech. But he wrote them down and handed it to us to read!

Though there were now many things we could no longer do together, he was still good company. Jerry and I were truly happy to have him around until he died at the age of ninety-three.

Not all patients are as easy to be with as my father. Some are unpleasant or ungrateful, or their physical care is more strenuous. All caregiving takes a toll on the family members who take it on. There's always added stress, lost privacy, and a strain on other relationships that also need one's attention. There will be at least some loss of freedom: an adult child or spouse may have to put a career or education on hold. Vacations may have to wait. And often there will be financial sacrifice.

Caring and Alzheimer's

But more and more, families are facing an even darker reality: caring for a loved one with Alzheimer's or another form of dementia. The statistics tell a devastating story. According to the Alzheimer's Association, in 2017 more than five million Americans were living with this disease. In 2016, 15.9 million family members and friends provided 18.2 billion hours of unpaid assistance.

Even so, total costs in 2017 were expected to reach $259 billion, with only 60 percent covered by Medicare and Medicaid. It's expected that more people will die from Alzheimer's or another dementia than breast and prostate cancer combined. Approximately two-thirds of caregivers are women. Approximately one-quarter are "sandwich generation" caregivers with children under the age of eighteen, 34 percent are age sixty-five or older, and 41 percent have a household income of $50,000 or less.[3]

In my home, I have cared for two close relatives with Alzheimer's and a friend with vascular dementia. The special vulnerability of an Alzheimer's patient demands additional emotional and spiritual resources from their loved ones. There are layers of shame, embarrassment, lies to protect the person's dignity, and personality and behavioral changes. Friends may avoid visits out of their own awkwardness or embarrassment, leaving both caregiver and patient feeling abandoned and isolated. Some behaviors involve personal hygiene or bathroom habits so distressing that one doesn't feel free to reveal them even to a support group. If the caregiver does talk about it, they may be dogged by a sense of betrayal.

Another unique aspect of caring for a loved one with dementia is what Dr. Pauline Boss in *Loving Someone Who Has Dementia* calls "ambiguous loss."[4] The person is both present and absent. He looks like your father or husband, but his personality has changed. A spouse who was always easygoing may become violent. One who was formerly engaged may become withdrawn or depressed. Behavior that is unpredictable keeps the caregiver on edge. Like a parent with a newborn, the caregiver can never completely relax.

When a spouse or parent dies, we can mourn and be supported by ritual and community. But with ambiguous loss there's no closure. One grieves in the present for the loved one, who is no more, and endures anticipatory grief for the ultimate separation through death. Since there is often a period of seven to ten years between diagnosis and death, such grief can become unbearable. A caregiver may shut down emotionally or begin to entertain thoughts they themselves believe morally unacceptable, such as abandonment, an affair, or even wishing for the other's death.

---

3. Taken from statistics provided by Alzheimer's Association, www.alz.org, July 3, 2017.

4. Pauline Boss, *Loving Someone Who Has Dementia* (San Francisco: Jossey-Bass, 2011).

Annette's Story

Annette (whose name has been changed here) is a close friend who cares for her husband. Mike began to show signs of dementia three years ago. He can still pass for normal in short social interchanges, but he is rapidly descending into mid-stage Alzheimer's. Annette, a committed Christian, gave me permission to share a little of her story:

> In my house my husband can tolerate talk about "memory loss" as long as you don't say it too often, but the A-word must never be spoken.
>
> Alzheimer's is worldwide. It can't be prevented or cured. And it eats at my table and sleeps in my bed. Little by little this invisible enemy is stealing my husband and my peace.
>
> The man I've loved for more than fifty years is becoming less and less like the man I live with. What does "till death do us part" mean when he's departing without dying? How do I find joy and peace? What does love look like now? Will I be able to be faithful to God, to my marriage, and to my own sense of integrity in the presence of this enemy? How much can I carry without losing my deepest self?

Here are some things Annette is learning to do in answer to her own questions:

> *I try to dwell in the present moment.* It's all I have. To dwell in the past is to be stuck in unresolved grief and longing. To obsess on the future is to dwell in fear. Things are manageable right this minute. I can cope—today. Mike and I still try to have a "date night" once a week, as we did when the kids were little. We like to eat out, then go to a concert or movie we can both enjoy.
>
> *Seize sparks of joy that spring up unexpectedly.* They are there if I just notice. For instance, this morning when the alarm went off I did not get up right away. I felt safe and loved in Mike's arms as we lay spoon fashion. I silently gave thanks for that moment.
>
> Later, Mike made a mess in the bathroom. I thought it was intentional and got mad. He said, "I can't seem to make you happy in the mornings."

It was the first time in ages he had even mentioned wanting to make me happy, and it surprised and touched me. I took his face in my hands, looked him in the eyes and said, "Honey, you made me happy this morning. I loved the way you were holding me." A happy smile spread across Mike's face. It told me he still wants to be close but is forgetting how. A moment of joy.

I try to create intimate moments. I also look for other ways to feel close. Yesterday I soaked Mike's feet, cut his toenails, and rubbed moisturizer on his dry legs. One of our daughters saw me and said, "Mom, that's an act of love." Yes, it was. And it felt good to both of us. Backrubs work too.

Annette does something else that many caregivers of spouses with dementia find critical to their own mental health: *She carves out space for a piece of life that is all her own.* She serves on the board of a charity she loves and teaches a class there from time to time. At least once a month, she goes to lunch with a professional colleague from her previous job, just to keep in touch with her professional identify. She needs something where she's recognized in her own right. These times can also produce moments of joy, if she remembers to notice.

Acceptance

Sometimes religious faith helps us accept what can't be changed. In *Abandonment to Divine Providence*, French Jesuit Jean Pierre DeCaussade wrote, "We must accept what we very often cannot avoid, and endure with love and resignation things which could cause us weariness and disgust. This is what it means to be holy."

Barbara is one of the gentlest, most peaceful people I know. Although she now has to dress and shave her husband Phil, and even brush his teeth, they walk to Mass together from their nearby apartment every day. She says, "Right now, taking care of Phil is my calling from God." Faith gives her life meaning and purpose.

Others, not so much. For Annette, wanting exactly what she has is still very hard. She doesn't believe that Alzheimer's—or cancer or any other ravaging disease—is God's will. The farthest she can go is this:

I ask God to help me behave in as loving a way as I can. When I don't feel affectionate, at least I will try to be kind. I ask for patience. And I ask God to give me strength to never abandon Mike. My desire is to help him live and die with dignity.

A writer friend of mine, married to a national hero, found her purpose in writing her husband's memoirs. She said, "I will be his memory."

Regardless of one's faith stance, caregiving is made easier by finding a path to peace with what is. As a prisoner in Auschwitz during World War II, Holocaust survivor Victor Frankl (*Man's Search for Meaning*) noticed that the inmates who lived longest were those who could articulate a larger purpose in their suffering. Frankl became convinced that a person can bear almost any "how" if they can find (or invent) a "why."[5] For the prisoners who succeeded, their extreme vulnerability became a vessel of hope.

Making peace with one's present reality is a process. It's a long walk through a dark wood. I don't have all the answers, but here are some thoughts on coming to accept our own or another's vulnerability:

Relinquish your idea of "how it's supposed to be." There has never been a perfect family, a perfect spouse, a perfect child, a perfect way to age, or a perfect death. Quit chasing perfection. Let it go. Some friends from Latin America taught me that "how it's supposed to be" is culturally conditioned. If I mentioned that Dad was living with us, American friends would say something like, "Oh, how kind of you to take him in!" As if I were a hero or a martyr. But friends from El Salvador and Peru and Mexico invariably said, "How lucky you are! I wish I could take care of my parents!" To them, I'd won the lottery. The cultural difference gave me a new perspective. With Dad, I did win the lottery.

You may have to redefine "love." Ancient Greeks had four words for it: *eros* is sexual love; *philia* is brotherly love or friendship between equals; *storge* is love between parents and children; and *agape* means good will, benevolence, the desire for the good of another.

---

5. Victor E. Frankl, *Man's Search for Meaning* (Boston: Beacon Press, 1959).

(In the New Testament, *agape* is used to express God's unconditional love.) As time passes, it may be that a*gape* endures when *eros* has weakened or even disappeared. Songwriter/poet Leonard Cohen called love "the holy or the broken hallelujah."

Focus on what's working, what's good, and then claim it. Dad was cheerful and appreciative. He loved life. He took up painting in his last three years and finished five canvasses. He taught himself Spanish and practiced with me. He read good books. Until he could no longer digest food, he'd accompany us to ethnic restaurants and try dishes he'd never before seen. Although caring for him did put a crimp in our love of travel or spending time at our beach house three hours from his doctor, helping him was worth that small sacrifice. Dad was grateful and so were we.

Nurture your own spirit. Write in a journal. Find a support group or a friend who will listen without trying to "fix" you or judge you. Talk about your feelings without blaming the patient or yourself. Listen to music that calms you or makes you feel happy. Read a book that inspires you. Pray, play, meditate, or walk in the woods. Embrace beauty.

We often look for vulnerability in others and try to hide our own. But our deepest pain is the very thing that makes us brothers and sisters with everyone we meet. It is our source of courage and growth. Our vulnerability comes bearing gifts—if we are only brave enough to receive them.

Part 2: Into the Woods, From Up Close and Afar

BY SIG

Most of you reading this will become or currently are a caregiver. According to the National Domestic Workers Alliance, 41.6 million Americans are caregivers: 56 percent are women, and 8.4 percent have children; 45 percent comprise the "sandwich generation, caring both for your children and your parents." On average you spend 3.2 hours per day providing unpaid care, and 62 percent of you are juggling full-time jobs—that is, if you're an onsite caregiver.[6]

It's possible instead that you may be providing care from a distance; you are what is called a long-distance or remote caregiver. Your parents may live several hundred miles away, in their own home (perhaps with help) or in one of three levels of a Continuing Care Retirement Community (CCRC): independent living, assisted living, or skilled nursing. Whether they are near or far, you could find yourself serving as their advocate, money manager, resource researcher or their only day-to-day human contact other than the professional caregiver you've hired to look out for them.

If you're like thousands of other remote caregivers, your parent or loved one is constantly on your mind. What if there's an emergency? What if she has an accident? A fire? A fall? That "Moment of Change" (as discussed in chapters 3 and 6) can happen any time. Nothing can make you feel more helpless than receiving a call from a hospital in another state: "Your father fell a few hours ago and broke his hip." By the time you've booked an airline ticket or driven overnight to your dad's town, the medical staff will have diagnosed his condition and begun treatment, maybe even a hip replacement. Expectations are that your dad will spend six weeks in rehab, and then he'll slowly regain his capacity to walk and resume his activities of daily living. But his Plan A is gone forever.

After checking in with Dad and reassuring him that you're going to be with him for a few days, it's time to don your patient

---

6. See www.caringacross.org, the website for the National Domestic Workers Alliance.

advocacy hat. When a medical professional is briefing you on his condition, you should ask whether he was *admitted* when the emergency team dropped him off or only held *for observation*.[7] This has nothing to do with whether Dad is sleeping overnight in a hospital or even what treatment he receives there. It has everything to do with whether Medicare will cover any subsequent costs of a stay in a rehabilitation facility.

Medicare normally does not pay for skilled nursing facility (SNF) care (often called "nursing homes"). But an important exception is this: If Dad was *admitted* for a "qualified hospital stay" of three days or more (not including discharge day), Medicare will cover expenses up to one hundred days in SNF for rehabilitation if prescribed by a doctor. Medicare pays nothing for an SNF after a hundred days (but may continue to pay for outpatient rehabilitation). But if Dad stays out of the hospital for sixty days after release from a SNF, and then is readmitted to a hospital for three days or more, a new period can begin.[8] If Dad was admitted only "for observation," regardless of how long he spent in the hospital even for a hip replacement operation, Medicare will not cover his rehab facility costs.

Carolyn learned this firsthand. When she broke her ankle in 2014, a three-hour surgery was required to piece her together with a plate and eight screws. Although the break required seven days in the hospital, Carolyn was "under observation" the entire time. When she transferred to a rehab center for another week, Medicare covered her physical therapy, medicine, and a walker, but she had to pay $1,100 a day for her stay in a shared room and meals.

My handicapped brother-in-law, who wears a huge brace on his left leg, had the same story although the ending was happier. When

---

7. As of March 8, 2017, through the Notice of Observation Treatment and Implication for Care Eligibility (NOTICE) Act, hospitals are required to notify patients who are under observation for more than twenty-four hours of their outpatient status within thirty-six hours or upon discharge if that occurs sooner. The act, however, does not require a hospital to change the patient's status.

8. Please do not treat this as legal advice. For up-to-date information, call Medicare toll-free at 1-800-638-6833.

he broke his "good" knee, he was never "admitted" to the hospital (though he stayed there for some days), so Medicare would not cover his rehab, but his secondary insurance coverage did. Somehow, the admissions social worker at the SNF (where he recuperated and received countless hours of physical and occupational therapy) arranged for his secondary policy to cover his stay—all of it. He was there for weeks. As long as the nursing home staff could attest that his condition was improving weekly, his secondary paid for everything but the television set in his room.

Importantly, improvement is not the standard by which Medicare will continue to cover patients in either SNF care or home health care after an "admitted" (not "for observation") inpatient hospital stay of three or more days (not including discharge day). A January 2013 court settlement (*Jimmo v. Sebelius*)[9] clarified Medicare policy and acknowledged that there may be specific instances where no improvement is expected in a patient's condition, but skilled care is nevertheless required in order to prevent or slow deterioration and maintain the patient (or beneficiary) at the maximum practicable level of function. Such coverage depends not on the beneficiary's restoration potential but on *whether skilled care is required*, along with the underlying reasonableness and necessity of the services themselves. Simply put, where skilled nursing care is required, whether in a SNF or at a Medicare-certified home health agency, *maintenance* trumps improvement in the patient's condition.

So, your next question to answer is: Does Dad have a Medicare supplementary insurance policy (commonly called secondary or Medigap insurance)? Since Medicare pays only 80 percent of non-hospital costs, many seniors have a secondary policy.[10] Most major insurance companies carry supplementary insurance, or approved plans are available through AARP.

---

9. See "*Jimmo v. Sebelius* Settlement Agreement Fact Sheet," https://www.cms.gov/Center/Special-Topic/Jimmo-Center.html. (Since the case was settled, there is no reported court decision.)

10. Carolyn's supplemental insurance covered her 20 percent but did not cover items that weren't covered under Medicare.

Back at the hospital with Dad: your next step is to meet with the hospital's social worker, who will create a discharge plan. This person can recommend rehab facilities near Dad's home and help you make knowledgeable choices based on location, cost, and services. They can also arrange for admission there and the next steps, such as transporting your father. They can be a source of immense help, a fount of unlimited knowledge, and your advocate. Be nice to them!

The hospital should have a copy of Dad's medical power of attorney. But it's possible that the ambulance workers who picked him up off the floor did not have time to search for the POA or Dad's meds, and he was too confused, scared, or maybe even unconscious, to be able to help. As mentioned in chapter 6, many people (not just seniors) have an envelope taped to their refrigerator door containing their health-care POA, list of meds, doctor's name and phone number, and their state's version of a "Do Not Resuscitate" form (if that's what they desire). EMS officers are trained to look there to see whether a victim has one.

If you have one or more siblings, when a crisis hits you'll want to confer with them immediately to share information and responsibility for Dad's care. Who will be his primary caregiver, and what roles will the others want to play?

Transparency: Keep Your Siblings in the Loop

You may talk with your parent daily or several times a week. If you're like most long-distance caregivers, you rarely bring up sensitive topics such as powers of attorney and health-care decision-making. But it's crucial that you (or one of your siblings) do talk about it, and that you share this information among yourselves. Whatever the distance, there's much you can do, especially if you have discussed your safety concerns with your parent. Here's a partial checklist for onsite and remote caregivers:

1. Do you have copies of your parents' powers of attorney (both health care and legal/financial)?

2. Have you discussed the contents of these documents with them and your siblings?

3. Do you know their doctors? How to contact them?

4. Do you have a list of their prescription medicines?

5. Do your parents keep you informed of their doctor appointments?

6. If they reside in any level of a CCRC, do you know the names and duties of the staff?

7. Do your parents have friends, or are they isolated?

8. Have you or your siblings inventoried senior resources in your parents' community?

While some parents remain secretive about their health concerns, we suspect that more often they really want you to know. Many live in isolation. Their friends have died or moved away, but your parents may resolutely insist on remaining in their own home or apartment. While you have tried and failed to persuade them to move to a continuing care community or to live with or near you, they refuse. That's all the more reason for you (and your siblings) to stay in the loop regarding their health, morale, and finances.

In such situations, sibling cooperation can actually affect a parent's health, for good or bad. What could be worse for a mother who lives in one locale than having to deal with adult children elsewhere who are competing to control her health-care, financial, and legal matters? It's enough she has to cope with the challenges that aging imposes. Squabbling children only make everything worse.

Siblings need to set aside their egos and resolve trust issues, if only for their parent's peace of mind. It's even better when they agree on a division of duties. For instance (with Dad's permission, of course), one child might follow his financial situation and another his health concerns. Throughout, sharing information (transparency) is key.

Say that on one of your visits you accompany Dad for his semi-annual physical checkup. You've accompanied him to these appointments for years, and your siblings never showed much interest. The examination was routine, and the doctor didn't detect anything currently serious. But the doctor recalls that Dad had walking pneumonia two months ago. He's recovered and resumed his daily activities. Should you share this information with your siblings before they learn about it in a subsequent phone call with your father? Absolutely! Telling your siblings right away *anything* new that you learn, whether financial or health related, will create trust among you and make it easier on Dad when an emergency strikes.

Another example: what if your sister, who lives closest to your mother (and is the primary sibling with caregiving responsibility), uses Mom's money to purchase a first-alert device or a home security system so she will know if Mom falls or needs help? You live several hundred miles away. Why should she bother telling you? *Because you care about your mom, too. Because knowing could give you more peace of mind. Because you might want to know how she's spending Mom's money.*

Too often what seems routine for one family member may appear as out of the ordinary for another. Questions bubble up such as: "How come I wasn't told about this?" "Why didn't you keep me in the loop?" or "How long has this been going on?" Worse: "You ingratiated yourself and turned Mom against me!"

What we've learned is simple: Take nothing for granted. View the situation from the other family member's perspectives. This is especially true for siblings who are dispersed throughout the country and probably feel some guilt that they're not more involved in their parent's life. *This is even truer with respect to money matters.* Keeping other family members in the dark, even innocently, can trigger suspicion, anger, and more than a dash of sibling rivalry.

Resources

Villages

How aware are you of local resources near your parents' home? Is there a senior center and, if yes, do they take advantage of it? Have you checked it out during visits to your parents? What about other resources your parents may either not know about or resist joining?

In many parts of the United States, the Village Movement is taking root. Villages are community-based membership organizations whose aim is to enable seniors to age in place for as long as medically feasible. No two villages are alike. Each has its own organic development and shapes its services to the needs and preferences of the members it serves.

Begun in Boston fifteen years ago, by 2017 some two hundred villages throughout the United States were helping seniors in myriad ways, such as transportation to doctors, grass cutting, snow shoveling, referrals to senior-friendly merchants, and other services. At the time of this writing, another one hundred fifty are being developed. In the Washington, DC, metropolitan area where I live, there are more than fifty-five villages, either fully operational or in development. Some villages have several hundred members and employ staffs comprising social workers, care coordinators, and hundreds of volunteers, many of them members themselves.[11]

PACE

Another program is PACE (Programs of All-Inclusive Care for the Elderly), a Medicare- and Medicaid-supported program that helps people meet their health-care needs in the community instead of going into a nursing home or other care facility.[12] If your parents are in a PACE program, they will have a team of health-care professionals working with them to make sure they receive the coordinated care they need. If your parents are enrolled in PACE, they may be required to use a PACE-preferred doctor. These doctors are best suited to help you make health-care decisions.

PACE organizations provide care and services in the home, the community, and the PACE center. Only thirty states, however, have PACE programs at this point. Many PACE participants receive most of their care from staff employed by the PACE. To qualify to join a PACE program, your parent must:

- Be fifty-five or older
- Live in the service area of a PACE organization

---

11. To learn more about Villages, see www.vtvnetwork.org.
12. To learn more about PACE, visit www.Medicare.gov and click on "PACE."

- Need a nursing home-level of care (as certified by your state)
- Be able to live safely in the community with help from PACE

Other Resources

Another good resource is Area Aging Centers. Since many seniors receive support from local, county, and state governments, Area Aging Centers provide an array of case management and other support services. In some jurisdictions, they offer free meals and transportation. More often than not, they provide support to mostly low-income seniors.

Even with all the existing resources, as the US aging population grows, more is needed to keep pace. You may be hard-pressed to identify senior services in your parent's community, and some you identify may be overtaxed with serving seniors who are in worse physical, psychological, or financial shape than your parents.

Getting outside Support

The time may come when your parent can no longer carry out all of their activities of daily living (ADL) on their own. Below are some signs to look out for.

Activities of Daily Living

Often referred to as self-care tasks, "Basic" ADLs include the following:

1. Taking prescribed medicines on time
2. Bathing or showering
3. Personal hygiene/grooming
4. Feeding oneself
5. Getting in and out of bed, moving from place to another (sometimes referred to as "functional mobility")
6. Dressing

"Instrumental" ADLs include the following:

1. Cleaning and maintaining one's home

2. Handling one's finances

3. Preparing meals

4. Shopping

5. Using a telephone

Say that on your most recent visit, you noticed Mom has lost weight, the refrigerator is half-empty, some food has rotted, and there's a pile of dirty clothes on the floor when usually her clothes are clean and neatly stored. If your parent can no longer maintain a safe and neat household or remember to bathe or take her prescription medicines on time, then you may have to consider hiring an aide.

Unless she lacks the appropriate mental capacity, the decision must be hers. You will need to have a conversation so she will accept help. But be prepared for some resistance. Why? She may deny she needs help because, like you, she treasures her autonomy. She may not want to spend the money. She may value her privacy and not want to share it—inviting a stranger into her home may feel like an intrusion, or even a violation; she may fear being robbed. Understandably, she doesn't want to cede control over her own life. Listen and let her know you value her dignity.

Like Carolyn with her dad, many adult children find it helpful to speak of their own needs. Say what you've noticed and that it worries you: "I wish I could help you more myself, but I'm not there. Just to relieve me, would you consider talking with someone who could tell us what's available?"

Aging Life Care Managers

That "someone" could be a geriatric care manager (now referred to as Aging Life Care Managers or ALCM) to evaluate your loved one's living conditions. While they are not MDs, most care managers have backgrounds in social work, gerontology, and nursing.

These professionals are equipped to assess the health, surroundings, and lifestyle of a client. They can facilitate discussions between you, your parent, and their medical professionals.

They can identify issues you may not spot: Is your mom's weight loss attributed to depression, side effects of her prescription medicines, or a digestive issue such as colon cancer? Are Dad's recent fender-benders due to vision loss or a neurological disorder such as incipient Parkinson's disease? Are your parents eating well? Are there ways the house could be made safer, such as getting rid of throw rugs and installing railings and grab bars where needed?

Licensed and certified by the Aging Life Care Association, their professional guild, they are trained to assess every aspect of an elder's lifestyle, health, and psychological functioning to help the family decide on the level of care needed. They can recommend services and typical costs. They can be engaged for a one-time evaluation or for ongoing supervision of employed caregivers.[13]

Choosing an Aide

Should your parent decide to hire an aide (with or without an assessment from an ALCM), how much outside support will Mom need *and agree to*? Is it just getting the housekeeping and laundry done? Or does it include getting dressed, preparing the day's main meal, grocery shopping, or bathing? Whether she hires an aide for one or two hours a day or for round-the-clock coverage, you should take time to explore local aging services that can refer you to an aide.

Many aides have the title Certified Nursing Assistant (CNA) or Patient Care Assistant (PCA). Some may not but are as experienced as a CNA or PCA. Check references. Typically, long-term care insurance will pay something for home health care but does require it to be by licensed professionals. (Check Mom's health policy if she has one.) Try to sit in as Mom interviews the person or participate by phone if you are out of town. *Attitude* is critical, because the aide has to be someone your parent will like.

---

13. To locate an ALCM in your area, visit www.aginglifecare.org.

Before reaching a contractual arrangement with an agency or with the aide directly, you'll want to assess the chemistry between your parent and the aide. Take your time, especially if you are a remote caregiver. Be sure Mom has ample opportunity to audition the aide herself before deciding on one. The last thing you want is a call in the middle of the night from your chronically ill or handicapped parent informing you she has fired her aide. Then you are back to square one. Aides can be miracle workers or demons. You want the former.

An effective aide should want to preserve as much of your parent's independence as possible. Where they can, they will give your mom the option to help herself and do things on her own terms. The aide should arrive on time, stay in regular contact with you, and inform you of any changes in your parent's condition. The aide becomes your radar.

The work of an aide can be backbreaking, repetitive, and demanding (and humiliating) especially in more intimate ways such as toileting and bathing. You will find that your mother's aide will likely turn out to be the one person most consistently in contact with her. Author and the director of the National Domestic Workers Alliance, Ai-Jen Poo, writes that aides "substantially cut health care costs by helping to manage chronic illnesses and by supporting people so that they can stay in their homes and out of radically more expensive institutions."[14]

Every state has its own regulations regarding aides. For example, most if not all states forbid an aide to administer prescription drugs. That's normally the responsibility of a Registered Nurse. However, an aide can lay out the medicine for the patient to self-administer. It pays to research this area as much as possible before engaging a full- or part-time aide.

Keep in mind that aides are some of the lowest paid workers in the United States. Most could never afford an aide of their own to care for their parents. While an agency that provides certified nursing assistants, or aides with lesser certification, may charge you $20–40 per hour, much less filters down to the aides themselves.

---

14. Ai-Jen Poo, *The Age of Dignity: Preparing for the Elder Boom in a Changing America* (New York: The New Press, 2015), 83.

The rest goes to the agency to cover costs and profit. According to www.1.salary.com, the average CNA earns just over $30,000 annually. A CNA who works in a long-term care residence may earn even less. And since most aides work irregular hours, it's questionable whether they receive benefits such as retirement and health coverage.

Managing Finances

Perhaps your parents' eyesight is dimming and keeping up with their bills is becoming more challenging. You live in another state and can't help with day-to-day financial matters. Daily Money Managers to the rescue! Daily Money Managers are trained, bonded, and certified professionals who will handle their bills and other financial matters on a personalized basis in their home. You no longer need to worry whether Mom or Dad is paying the bills on time or in full.

According to their professional standards, the Daily Money Managers help with bill paying and preparing budgets, among other services, for seniors and older adults, people with disabilities, busy professionals, high-net-worth individuals, small businesses, and others. Their mission is to support daily money management services in an ethical manner, to provide information and education to members and the public, and to develop a network of dedicated professionals.[15]

An Alternative to Institutional Care

At some point your parent may need more care than an aide can provide. Before looking into institutional care, however, you should first check out a feature of Medicaid of which most Americans are unaware. When we think of Medicaid for older adults, we usually assume a government-supported program that pays for qualified low- or no-income seniors in skilled nursing residences. Many families spend years trying to qualify a chronically ill parent or loved one for Medicaid-covered skilled nursing.

---

15. You can find more information on this resource at www.aadmm.com.

In 1981, congress approved legislation allowing states and the District of Columbia (DC) to offer alternatives to institutional care. Referred to as "home and community based care," a broad array of medical and nonmedical services (excluding room and board) may be provided by the states and DC to both disabled and elderly persons who are not otherwise covered under Medicaid. Depending on the jurisdiction, these might include:

- Respite relief for a caregiver[16]

- Home health aide

- Assistive technology services

- Modifications to the home that incorporate wider doors, ramps, or roll-in showers for wheelchair-bound persons

- Communication aids (such as speech amplifiers)

- Even guide dogs

Passage of this statute represented a first step toward recognizing that many individuals can be supported in their homes and communities, thereby preserving their independence and bonds to family and friends, at a cost usually less than institutional care.[17]

Choosing the Right Institutional Care

The time may come, however, when your parent may require assisted living or skilled nursing care. Before Mom (and you) decides to take that step, consider the following measures.

First, if a doctor recommends either full-time at-home care or institutional care, *seek a second opinion from another medical professional.* When my mother's doctor said her condition warranted round-the-clock care, she took him at his word. I wish she had requested a second (or even a third) opinion. Some seniors consider their doctors to be demigods and follow their advice to the letter. My mother was one of those.

---

16. Medicare offers up to five days of paid respite care to a caregiver with a patient receiving hospice care at home.

17. For more state-by-state information, see www.medicaidwaiver.org.

In a matter of days we secured a pleasant, safe, and well-managed (or so we thought) assisted living arrangement. From the day she arrived there, she was unhappy. I'll never be sure, but a more positive second opinion might have might have made her remaining years less despondent.

Second, talk to others residing there. *And try to talk with their adult children.* That's another task I wish we'd done before Mom moved into her assisted living residence. Other residents' family members will usually give you an unvarnished appraisal of a facility's staff, service, and accommodations. They'll warn you what to look out for. If you haven't the time or inclination, do an Internet search (www.yelp.com was helpful for me) for assisted living residences in your area.

Third, spend some time at the residence. Most will invite you to have lunch at their facility as part of their marketing effort. Is the dining room attractively furnished? Do the residents seem pleasantly engaged? How is the food and the staff serving it? Do you feel some rapport between residents and staff? As you explore the premises, do you see activities and programs for the residents? What kind of recreational space does it have? What about a garden that residents can tend? At my mother's place, there was only a small "recreational" room with a rabbit and some arts and crafts materials. The recreation director scheduled few programs for the residents.

Fourth, is it a resident-centered (or staff-centered) residence? (Look for the former.) Do the residents (in independent or assisted living) have an opportunity to voice their concerns, complaints, and expectations in monthly or more frequent meetings? Do they have access to senior staff so they can discuss their issues privately? While some residents may be satisfied with whatever they're provided, others want to feel engaged in planning activities or commenting on the quality of food, service, and accommodations. After all, it's now their home. A resident-centered facility provides for resident input and evaluation and recognizes the dignity and autonomy of the people it serves.

Fifth, moving into a CCRC—be it independent, assisted living, or skilled nursing—is physically and emotionally challenging. Downsizing hurts. For some, the move is traumatic. If your parent is in that category, be available on the phone, for additional visits, and in other ways to ease their adjustment to the new surroundings. It may take time.

Other older adults are delighted not to cope with laundry, meal preparation, and housekeeping chores. For them, weekly meet-and-greets and other ice-breakers make for a soft landing. Activities might include a bridge club, weekly outings to recreational areas, and special events. Guest speakers satisfy the interests of many residents. A good residence is one that welcomes them, wherever they are on the emotional map, and helps them feel comfortable in their new surroundings.

Finally, finances. Perhaps the biggest question is how to pay for residential care. Long-term care insurance coverage may pay only for skilled nursing care (not assisted living), and even then, nothing for the first ninety or one hundred days depending on the type of policy. In any event, it's unlikely it will cover the full monthly charge. Many residents sell their family home when they move out. Sometimes children chip in to pay Mom's or Dad's expenses. Medicaid (not Medicare) requires personal impoverishment before one is eligible.[18] Most assisted living residences ramp up monthly charges as a resident requires help with a growing number of activities of daily living. Make sure you understand the residence's billing system before your parent moves in and as your parent's care needs increase.

Guardianship

What happens if you, acting as your parents' (remote or onsite) caregiver, die or can no longer carry out your responsibilities? There is no close family member or friend willing to serve as your surrogate. You are "the one and only." This happened to Donald, an acquaintance of mine.

---

18. Financial planners specializing in elder law may be able to suggest ways, such as irrevocable trusts and annuities, to protect a portion of one's assets and still be eligible for Medicaid. See, for example, https://www.felintonlaw .com/estate-planning-medicaid/.

His attorney informed him: "Well, if you die before your [aging, homebound] sister Gabriela does, then she'll need a guardian." The attorney's remark was like a punch in the gut. Gabriela relied on Donald to handle her financial, health care, and other concerns. He realized that no one who lived near her could be trusted or would be willing to handle her needs. His sister could, in effect, end up becoming a ward of the state.

If no family member can serve as guardian, then a local court normally appoints a qualified attorney to serve. The court charges them with care and management of a person (or an estate, or both) deemed no longer competent to manage their own affairs. Guardians hold immense power. They can remove all or most of an adult's decision-making authority. Although they do not hold legal title to a ward's property, they can prevent their ward from entering into a contract regarding the property, such as selling the family home or using a portion of their savings for travel. (In some jurisdictions, a person with authority to control the ward's money or real estate is called a *conservator*. In others, the guardian may have authority over both the person and their possessions.)

If Gabriela is not completely lucid she will likely have no say about where she lives, how her resources are spent, or maintaining her health care. Guardians are expected to act in the best interest of their ward and are accountable to the court that appointed them. According to studies cited by the Quality Trust for Individuals with Disabilities,[19] the number of adults under guardianship has tripled since 1995: 90 percent of public guardianship cases have resulted in a guardian being empowered to make *all decisions* for the person.

If you are in a situation similar to Donald's, it behooves you to check out alternatives to guardianship. Your parent or close relative may have retained sufficient capacity to take part in some decision-making. An all-or-nothing approach such as guardianship may result in isolation, depression, or worse. Studies show that guardianship—however liberal—can impose drastic restraints on an individual's liberty and, according to one source, result in an individual having fewer rights than a convicted felon.

---

19. See www.dcqualitytrust.org (see also below).

One alternative to guardianship is Supported Decision Making (SDM).[20] This approach recognizes a person's autonomy and her capacity to take part in decision-making in a way that does not remove all of her rights. SDM allows a person with a disability to use friends, family members, professionals, and a network of other trusted persons in making her own decisions. These "supporters" help the person understand issues and choices, ask questions, receive explanations in understandable language, and communicate decisions to others.

A Supported Decision Making arrangement recognizes that mental capacity is not black and white—it is a *continuum*. A person may be able to make some decisions but not others. For example, consenting to a flu shot requires a different level of decision-making skill than consenting to open-heart surgery. Capacity also may change over time based on the person's experience or the situation. Lacking the opportunity to make decisions can prevent one from developing or maintaining capacity.

In the District of Columbia, where I reside, the law calls for courts to encourage maximum self-reliance and independence of people found to be incapacitated and to appoint the least restrictive type of guardianship.[21] In the case of Donald, however, his sister lacked sufficient capacity to manage her financial, physical, and social well-being. Even with outside support, she needed someone else to make decisions for her, either through a guardianship or maybe a power of attorney.

Wrapping Up

We hope we have prepared you for the joy, the pain, the challenge, and the reward of caregiving as your parents grow more vulnerable. Most of what you've read is based on our own or our

---

20. Three US case rulings undergird this innovative and humane treatment of such individuals: In re Perry, 727A.2d 539 (Pa. 1999); in re Dameris L., 956 N.Y.S. 2d 848 (N.Y. Sur. Ct. 2012); and *Ross v. Hatch*, No. CWF 120000426P-03 (Va. Cir. Ct. 2013).

21. The Quality Trust for Individuals with Disabilities in Washington, DC, provided some material in this section; see www.qualitytrustdc.org.

friends' and clients' experience. While we urge you to be prepared for this awesome responsibility, in some ways preparedness can be impossible. We all react to change differently. We cannot predict how we will control our emotions under pressure, unleash our energy after hours of caring, and encounter unanticipated events each new day. Here is our advice:

1. *Take care of yourself.* Airlines tell passengers, "Put on your own oxygen masks before helping your child." Although this seems counterintuitive, it's true. As critical as your responsibilities are to another, equally important is your obligation to stay healthy, in contact with others, and able to ask for assistance. Look for agencies, friends, or family members who will offer respite care, if only to give you a few free hours, a day, or even a week.[22]

2. *Take advantage of as many resources as you can.* We've listed some in the Resources Guide at the end of this book, but there are countless more. Ask questions. If necessary, be a nag! You're navigating a huge vessel; you deserve all the aid you can get.

3. As a current or future caregiver—onsite or remote—*be transparent with other family members.* You need one another. In these situations, TMI (Too Much Information!) can be a virtue. If you are not the primary caregiver in your family, step up. Listen to the one who is. Hear their worries, hopes, and expectations. Offer to help.

4. Finally, *think of your tasks as gifts.* You may not be in a gift-giving mood, but to the care recipient, that's who you are: The Gift.

---

22. If your loved one qualifies for hospice, Medicare will provide for five days' respite care in an approved facility.

8

Letting Go: The Path to Freedom

by Carolyn

"Everything I've ever let go of has claw marks on it."

Anne Lamott

When the Weather Channel predicted a frigid winter ahead, Judy Jones knew she had to try one more time. This was not a professional problem from her work as a geriatric care manager at a senior service agency in Washington, DC. This was personal.

Judy's parents lived on a hill with a steep driveway that iced over when the mercury fell. She knew it was dangerous, all the more as they grew older. During the winter, they could be literally trapped for days at a time.

But Judy's father, a retired naval captain, blew up when his daughter suggested—again—that it might be time for him and her mother to move into a retirement community. Judy made every rational argument she could summon, showed them photos of lovely, safe communities, and offered to take them to lunch at several. The captain would have none of it. "We're not moving!" he barked.

Finally she screwed up her courage and asked, "Dad, could you just tell me why you and Mom won't move?"

"We can't."

"Why can't you?" Judy persisted.

"We have too much stuff. We'll have to stay here till we die."

Oh, Judy thought. *It wasn't blind stubbornness or even attachment to their home that was stopping them. It was feeling overwhelmed at the thought of getting rid of their stuff!* Judy's parents were not only trapped by the snow. They were trapped by their possessions.

She said, "Look, Dad. When you and Mom pass, my sister and I will have to go through all this stuff and clear out the house. Let us do it now. That way we can all do it together, and you and Mom can help us decide what to keep." She added as an afterthought, "It would be a lot easier on us girls."

Two weeks later, the captain announced that he and his wife were moving. "He" had found a perfect retirement community.

When I looked around my house, I knew how the captain felt. I was staring at ten rooms and a garage full of stuff accumulated over fifty-six years of marriage. The last time we'd moved was twenty-eight years earlier—and even then we'd brought some unsorted boxes with us. Later on, my parents lived with us until they died, and I still had boxes of their photos, letters, and birthday cards brought with them from Florida and never opened since they moved in here.

My husband Jerry died in 2015, and in early 2017 I sold our house and moved into a condo half its size. I was helped by the thought of sparing my children the painful chore of throwing away my left-behinds. But, like the captain, I needed them to help me actually do it. Fortunately, they were willing.

Sister Jose's Simplicity

That I may have a small problem did not dawn on me with this morning's sunrise. Some fifteen years ago I had signed up for a three-day workshop on "How to Simplify Your Life." It was led by a Franciscan nun and writer, Sister Jose Hobday, a tall, powerfully built woman with a warm smile that contradicted a no-nonsense air. Born of a Seneca-Iroquois mother and an Anglo Southern Baptist father, she was the only girl in a family of eleven children. She was both a Seneca elder and a Franciscan nun. Her attitude toward "stuff" was shockingly countercultural.

Sister Jose could fit nearly everything she owned into a suitcase. She traveled the world with only a backpack. She had two dresses she had made herself, identical sleeveless shifts that reached mid-calf, which she wore plain in summer and over a long-sleeved sweater or turtleneck, jumper fashion, in winter. She reasoned that she could only wear one at a time, so she'd never need more than two: one to wear while the other was being washed. She wore sandals on her feet, adding heavy socks in winter. She must have had a coat or a blanket, but I didn't see it because I met her in summertime.

She explained that things were not to be acquired but to be used for good and, when no longer needed, given away. She and some other Franciscan nuns lived in a house in a poor neighborhood. Since they had so few possessions, they had never locked their door—until someone gave them a computer. Almost immediately it disappeared. The donor offered to replace it on condition they'd lock it up at night. The nuns grieved. They complied because they needed the computer, but locking the door felt like a little death.

Sister Jose almost made getting rid of stuff sound like fun. "Things take up a lot of energy," she said. "You have to dust them and wash them and polish them and guard them and repair them when they break. You have to insure them and hunt for them when they get lost. Having stuff makes you anxious." And by the way, she reminded us, "stuff" takes up space a needy stranger might occupy.

Her only exception was books. Sister Jose allowed herself to have fifty, including a Bible. This meant if she acquired a new one, even as a gift, she had to give one away. She admitted that was hard.

At the close of the workshop, she challenged us. "Think about one thing you're spending time on that you don't really care about. You only do it to please or impress others. Strike a blow for freedom! Just quit!"

Instantly I knew what I would give up. That was the day I stopped coloring my hair.

Can Downsizing Be Fun?

If I know it's the road to freedom, why then do I find it so hard—terrifying almost—to think about detaching from my stuff?

For one thing, I'm a creature of my culture—and in America downward mobility is deeply countercultural. We admire Mother Theresa, but success in our country is usually measured by acquiring more and more. It's a mark of maturity—and a great blessing—to know how much is enough.

"He who dies with the most toys wins." That's what the bumper sticker said. As a young person, I knew that statement was untrue but couldn't articulate why. Then I saw another version of the same one. Someone had put a line through "wins" and written "dies."

So how do I loosen my grip on my "toys"? I'm trying to reframe the process, not as losing things but gaining space. Clutter is not pretty. There may be a thin line between clutter and hoarding. If you can no longer walk through every room in your house, sit on all your furniture, and use the bathtub to take a bath, you're probably hoarding. If you are, then you need professional help. Hoarding is a serious problem and not one you can easily fix by yourself. Thankfully, I'm not there yet. But even in my new space, I'm seeing stuff begin to collect.

Here's what I did. I started small. Cleaning out a kitchen desk drawer actually feels deeply satisfying. The easy part is throwing away old magazines or giving away unworn clothes. Books are a little harder—I can't foresee the time I'll get down to fifty, but maybe two hundred? It does give me more than a twinge to recognize that I'll have to sell the china and silver serving dishes lovingly collected from around the world, because none of my kids wants them and there's no room in my new space.

Values and Culture

A catastrophic weather event or a national tragedy such as 9/11 reveals the hidden values that lie deep within each of us: love for our families, compassion for our neighbors, empathy with the suffering. Even willingness to risk our lives to save others.

Why are these values hidden? Blame it on the unexamined cultural assumptions imbibed with our mother's milk. When we're young our parents teach us to compete, to achieve, to climb the ladder. In middle age, advertisers urge us to stimulate the economy by spending lavishly, accumulating more and better and newer. We're creating jobs. It's patriotic. When we get too old (or too wise) to compete or accumulate, we're expected to quietly fade away.

Why do we accept these values? It is because they hide behind (and support) the personas we wear in public. They satisfy our need to feel important and independent. They buoy up our ego. Their shallow nature may remain invisible until the mask is ripped off by a life-shattering experience such as a catastrophic fire, a cancer diagnosis, or the death of a loved one. Then we're brought face to face with what really matters.

And we know it when we see it.

In his book *The Road to Character*, author and social commentator David Brooks urges us to let go of what he calls "résumé virtues" and focus on developing "eulogy virtues." Résumé virtues are marks of achievement: education, job titles, talents others recognize. Things that show I'm smart and capable. Marks of recognition that stroke my ego.

Eulogy virtues are the things people talk about at funerals: generosity, kindness, courage, honesty, faithfulness—*values that focus on relationships with others.* The eulogy virtues are other words for love.

"So-wa-ha!"

I once read that Hindus have a spiritual practice to prepare for losses, up to and including life itself. This exercise is useful because it foresees symbolically what we all will experience if we live to old age. Try it. It's harder than it sounds.

You envision a huge bonfire. With a loud cry, "*So-wa-ha!*" you imagine throwing into the fire, one at a time, everything that binds you to the earth. You begin with possessions, working up to those most difficult to relinquish. My books. My baby grand piano. *So-wa-ha!* You move to your work, then relationships, and finally your own body. How is it even possible to let go of these? But the reality is that eventually we will lose them all.

A Dream Deferred

When we're young, our work may be our primary identity. It may feed our egos but also truly help others. We love what we do. Imagine, then, how it will feel to be forced out by health, age, or an economic downturn. Who will I be when I'm too old to practice law or mediate disputes? I hate to whine, but it feels like a small death. I'm being stripped bare. *So-wa-ha!*

But there's a sense in which letting go now can reap a blessing in the future. It may mean looking backward to pick up a dream deferred.

In our fifties and into our sixties, some of us will be at the height of our careers. We may be workaholics, stressed out, drink too much, and ignore our families. Then, boom! The time comes for us to retire and we wonder, "What's next? Who am I now?" This can feel unbearable—or it can bring freedom to pursue a road less traveled.

Here's a version that's common to women: postponement or interruption of a career for full-time motherhood. Or we follow a husband across the country when he gets an offer he can't refuse. Or we become full-time caregiver of a parent with Alzheimer's. Your dreams go on ice—maybe for a long time. Women know what it is to let go—and wait.

Letting go is painful. But closing one door can open others. You may discover talents you never knew you had. And you may also help your family and others in the process.

Carolyn's Deferred Dream(s)

This was my weird and unplanned trajectory: grad school, teaching, wife-ing, and mom-ing. Unconsciously, I was preparing for a yet unseen time when I'd be able to do "my own thing," whatever that was. As a full-time homemaker, I took correspondence school writing classes (I sold three pieces). Got certified as a volunteer community arbitrator. Played guitar and sang in a country band connected with my church. Stuffed envelopes and called voters for a political candidate.

All this time, the women's movement was being born. And I was paying attention. For fourteen years, though, I let go of my own ambitions and supported my husband's career and our children's activities until they were in middle school.

Then it seemed possible to take up my deferred dream. Fourteen years after graduating from college, I started law school, graduated, and became a trial lawyer, and eight years later I became a judge. As my children grew up and left home, I let go of them with as much grace as I could muster. Then I retired and let go again of the status of being "Judge Parr" and became "Carolyn" to homeless men with AIDS at Joseph's House and "Carolina" to immigrant moms at The Family Place. Now I write and help people resolve disputes without going to court. I think of it as a call to peacemaking.

I've worn a lot of hats. They have all been deeply satisfying, one at a time. I would never have been equipped to do the things I most enjoy now if I had not been able to let go of my earlier passions. And who knows what's next?

Right now the moment is in the future, but I know it's coming: I may well outlive my ability to work. Who will I be then? I should begin to prepare myself inwardly. So should we all.

From letting go of work, we move to relationships—those that are life-giving and those that challenge our very identity. We can let painful relationships go, by looking backward with forgiveness to find freedom in the present. Back then, we knew only part of the story, how someone else's behavior affected us. By reflecting now on what we didn't know then (about the other person's burden, motivation, fear), we can try to walk in the other's shoes. We can reframe our judgment of the person. We can do this even if the person has died.

We often hear, "You can't change the past." That's true in one sense. The "facts" of any story may be clear and unalterable. But meaning is not found in the facts. The meaning lies in the life experiences we bring to the facts and the interpretation we take away. There is a way to loosen the grip of a bitter memory: it's called reframing.

"Reframing" Mama

Reflecting on a painful experience can give it a new meaning. Like an old family photo, changing the frame changes how the picture looks. New details emerge into awareness. A new frame opens possibilities for forgiveness and reconciliation, for personal growth, and for moving on from a hard stuck place.

A few years ago, I wrote my spiritual autobiography to fulfill a requirement for ordination. In the process, I reflected on painful memories that kept me bound to the past in unhealthy ways. At first I asked myself, "Why did this happen?" But then I realized that was the wrong question. Only God knows why bad things happen. The more helpful questions for me were, "What can I learn from that? How can I grow from it? How can I work with God to use it to help others?"

Those are still good questions when the stuff hits the fan.

The deepest sadness of my life was that my mother and I never bonded. When I was born, my father was unemployed and my parents were living with his parents in a tiny overcrowded house. The Great Depression was not a good time to have a baby.

My mother was a pretty woman, but from early childhood I remember the disapproval in her dark brown eyes. I remember her tightly pursed lips that seldom kissed me. She did her motherly duty as she saw it, which included liberal spankings, most of which I did not deserve. I could sometimes win her approval by making good grades and getting recognition from others, but I never in all my life felt she loved me. (I did feel loved by my father and grandmother and aunt, so the absence of Mama's affection was painful but not emotionally fatal.)

By the age of six, I'd given up seeking her affection. And as a teenager, I really didn't like her very much. I thought she was lazy. Although she had been a teacher and social worker before I was born and until I was three, she did not work outside the home again until I left for college. After my younger sisters started going to school, I could never figure out what Mama did all day. Every single afternoon when I came home the house was a mess and she'd be taking a nap.

We could have used an extra paycheck. Dad was a carpenter, and money was always a struggle. We never had a washing machine like the other neighbors because Mama didn't want to do laundry. Dad's work clothes and our sheets and towels were picked up by a cleaning service and delivered the next week. I learned to wash and iron my own school outfits. Later, Mama washed my sisters' dresses, but until they were bigger they wore them to school wrinkled unless I ironed them. I often did it out of embarrassment and pity, secretly fuming. Mama was always "too tired." *Doing what?* I wondered.

She bought vitamins from a door-to-door salesman and visited doctors often, though nothing improved. I secretly thought she was a hypochondriac, squandering the money Dad sweated to earn in the Miami sun. I was full of judgment. I secretly fantasized that she and Dad would divorce, I'd live with him, and he'd find a new wife who would love me.

Not until I worked on my spiritual memoir did I realize Mama was probably clinically depressed. One day, long after I was grown up, she confided that the only time her father ever touched her was to put his hand on her forehead to check if she had a fever when she was sick. I suddenly understood why she liked to visit doctors.

These two revelations, her depression and deprivation of a father's touch, freed me to see my mother in a new light. And something else happened. One day I was in the car alone with Mama when out of the blue she said, "Daddy says you don't think I love you. Did you ever think that?" (Thankfully, she did not follow up with, "But I do." Truth-telling was one of her core values.)

The question shocked me. I recognized Mama was making herself vulnerable in that moment and I had no desire to go on the attack. But I wanted to answer honestly. After a pause I said, "Well, when I was little, I saw that other mothers would kiss and hug their children. You hardly ever touched me."

She sighed. "When you were nine, one of the neighbors noticed that and asked me about it." Her voice broke. "I don't know why I didn't. I just couldn't." And finally, "I wasn't much of a mother."

It might seem hard to hear your mother say she couldn't touch you. But it freed me to know I hadn't imagined this. And I wasn't to blame.

I said, "Mama, I think you did the best you could."

It was true. Being who she was, she did the best she could. That was as close as she could come to an apology, but it was enough. In that moment I forgave her.

Mama and I never did develop a touchy-feely relationship, but when she was in her nineties with Alzheimer's, I helped Daddy care for her in my home. And I was glad to be able to do it.

So-wa-ha!

Letting Go of Those We Love

I'm most bound to the earth by the people I love. I can't even try to imagine throwing those relationships into the bonfire. The closest I can come is to imagine releasing them to God.

This is perhaps the hardest letting go: Allowing a loved one to die when they choose to die—not when a medical professional deems it appropriate, or when a family member wants a close and cherished loved one to "hang on" longer.

My friend Amparo died much too young from breast cancer that metastasized to her spine. She was in agony. I could not in good conscience beg her to linger. She said, "God and I are having a serious conversation." She smiled.

For days, her husband Edgar stayed at her bedside reading to her, urging her to sip the chicken soup he'd made and brought from home. It was devastating for him and their children to think about never seeing their mother again on this side of heaven. But finally they knew they had to release her. She had suffered enough, and she was ready.

We can't predict who, but the chances are overwhelming that we will surely say goodbye to someone we love before we ourselves pass. We will grieve.

In *Final Gifts*, authors and hospice nurses Maggie Callahan and Patricia Kelley write, "In ways that are direct or subtle or even silent, dying people are showing us that they DO know when their deaths will occur and that they are not distressed by this information."[1]

My husband Jerry died from heart failure at the age of eighty-five, just three days short of our fifty-sixth wedding anniversary. He had lost thirty pounds in the past two months; he could not or would not eat more than a bite of anything, though he did drink water and juice. I tried to coax him to eat and he wanted to please me, but he had trouble swallowing and nothing increased his appetite. He denied anything was wrong and said he planned to live to one hundred.

---

1. Maggie Callahan and Patricia Kelley, *Final Gifts, Understanding the Special Awareness, Needs, and Communications of the Dying* (New York: Simon & Schuster, 1992), 124.

Finally a friend who had been a hospice chaplain said, "Carolyn, Jerry's body may be shutting down. Hospice tells us to offer food but to accept no for an answer if a patient refuses it. He's not trying to starve himself. His digestive system may be giving up along with his heart and kidneys." She was right. When I relaxed, Jerry's anxiety seemed to lift.

In his last two weeks of life, he accepted that he was dying and he let me know. Like a davening pilgrim at Jerusalem's Wailing Wall, Jerry began to rock back and forth, making a mournful sound with words I could not understand.

"Honey, are you in pain?" I asked.

"No."

"Are you praying?"

"Yes."

"Does it comfort you to rock back and forth?" I said, trying to understand.

"Yes." And then, so softly I had to move up close to hear, "You know, it's not really so bad. It's not bad at all." He started to hum a familiar children's hymn, "Jesus Loves Me."

A few hours later I noticed Jerry's lips were moving, so I edged up closer on the sofa to try to hear. Unaware of me, rocking, eyes shut, hands open, he was whispering, "Thank you. Thank you. Thank you."

There were still times when he wanted to stay, but he was getting ready to leave.

Callahan and Kelley share countless stories about terminally ill persons, who in one manner or another let loved ones know whether they had unfinished business to resolve before dying. By being aware of and respecting their words and expressions, we can understand these messages, as well as how we can make their next journey easier.

But how can we decode these messages? Some people want to talk about love or forgiveness or God or what's on the other side. Others, not so much. Until nearly the very end, my father met any efforts to open a deeper level of conversation with "So where are the Redskins in the Super Bowl playoffs?" Alex Shearer says that maybe the message from those like Dad is, "I'm not dead yet. I'm still a part of life."[2]

There's no one way that's right for everybody. Some want desperately to stay, like Dad, even though he was ninety-three years old and devoured by prostate cancer. Others are ready to go but need a loved one's permission. We should follow the lead of the dying person.

My husband's colleague Wilt had invited Jerry and me to come to his home to speak with his dying wife. Kayla was sitting upright on the sofa in her living room. She was attached to an oxygen tank. A swollen leg, where fluid pooled from heart failure, was propped up. She described how sad she was not to be able to see her grandchildren grow up. Then she asked, "How do you do it?" We didn't understand. Kayla tried again. "How do you let go?"

I thought for a minute and responded with a gentle question of my own. "What's holding you here?"

She silently turned her head toward her husband as if asking for help.

I understood. "Wilt, are you able to let her go?"

He took a breath, looked at her tenderly, and said, "Yes." Then he confessed, "Every night before she goes to sleep I've been begging her, 'Just hold on until morning.' Now I realize that was wrong." Eyes filling, he took her hand and said, "Honey, I know you need to go. It's okay to go. I'll be all right."

Kayla died in her sleep that night.

A Word about Grief

Everybody grieves differently.[3] Some survivors seem to never get over a serious loss, including the loss of a loved one. When Jerry died, I learned that even the darkness of grief, like vulnerability, comes with gifts if we are able to accept them.

The gift of tears. I was conditioned as a child not to cry, and I seldom do. With Jerry's death, I became acquainted with wrack-

---

2. Alex Shearer, *This Is the Life* (New York: Simon & Schuster, 2014), 206.
3. One of the most helpful books about grief is Ann Kaiser Stearn's *Living through Personal Crisis* (Enumclaw, WA: Idyll Arbor, 2010).

ing, gut-wrenching sobs that began in the belly, rose up my throat, and spilled from my eyes. Though the sobbing abated after a few months, weeping relieved the anguish and reminded me of how much I had loved Jerry for fifty-six years. It reassured me that I have a heart of flesh.

The gift of old friends. While Jerry was alive, Roscoe, an old friend from Jerry's boyhood, sent him DVDs and CDs of music they'd listened to together when they were young. (Now Roscoe sends me purple-topped turnips he grows himself and books he knows I'll like.) More than forty-five of Jerry's former colleagues visited him in his last two months of life. He knew each one and was buoyed by their love. "I know they're coming to say goodbye," Jerry said after one visit. But he was puzzled. "I can't understand why they seem to *love* me so much."

The gift of stories. Though Jerry had no idea, I learned why people loved him so much. They told me—face to face and in phone calls, letters, and e-mails. The stories rolled in. Stories of how Jerry had changed their lives—stories from famous people such as Nancy Reagan, and from humble folk such as recovering addicts where Jerry volunteered at Samaritan Inns. One man sent me a copy of a reference letter Jerry had written that helped him get promoted *thirty years earlier.* A Secret Service colleague told of a book Jerry sent him when his fourteen-year-old son died in 1984. One after another, witnesses testified to their gratitude for specific kind acts that still lived in their hearts. Some called him "the best boss I ever had." They mentioned his humility, sense of humor, integrity, compassion, decency, and praised his example. A speaker at Jerry's memorial even lauded Jerry's vulnerability. These stories brought me deep joy.

The gift of presence. Grief brought our family even closer. Daughters, sons-in-law, and sisters rallied around. Neighbors dropped in with food. When Jerry became too weak to go to church, our little faith community met in our home. Members and colleagues pitched in when our paid helpers were off; later they handled all the funeral logistics. Food, flowers, and donations to named charities poured in. We are grateful beyond the telling.

These unexpected gifts of grief made it easier to let it go. "Thank you. Thank you. Thank you."

Talking to Grief

What can you say to the parent of a seventeen-year-old son who dove into a wave this summer and came up paraplegic? Or your fifty-three-year-old family member who suddenly discovered he is riddled with cancer? Or a church friend who is helplessly watching her husband's slow but unstoppable surrender to dementia and death?

"Get Well Soon" cards don't touch the situations of heartbreaking, ongoing loss, though recipients might recognize the care behind the card. Below are some consoling words, however, that really do feel helpful.

Encouragement. The injured teenager (or a wounded warrior) needs words of encouragement. View the setback as a challenge. Encourage your friend to remain positive, affirm his inner resolve and resilience. He's a survivor. Helpful words are *courage, strength,* and *hope.* If a complete cure is not possible, then speak of hope for a meaningful future.

Spiritual Help. Whether someone considers themselves religious or not, wishes for peace, hope, and comfort are still meaningful. A Hallmark card expresses a hope for "moments of grace when you need them most." For people of faith a simple "I'm praying for you" (or "sending loving thoughts your way") can be helpful. Scripture quotations may be comforting: "Nothing can separate us from the love of God" (Romans 8), or "To everything there is a season" (Ecclesiastes 3).

Reveal your own vulnerability. "I hardly know what to do or say. This must be so hard for you." Indeed, as one Hallmark card said, "Illness can shake up your world in a way that little else can." As a friend, you may feel helpless in the face of a situation that can't be fixed. Winnie the Pooh told Rabbit, "A friend is someone who helps you up when you're down, and if they can't, they lay down beside you and listen." A hug or holding hands does not require words.

Say, "You are not alone." People who are terminally ill often feel abandoned or isolated, as do their families. It's critical to remind them that others care, that they are surrounded with love and being held in the light. Visit often, for your simple presence shows you care. Offer a few hours to give the caregiver a break. Say, "We're all thinking of you." Once when I was very sick, I confessed to a friend that I found it hard to pray for myself. He said, "Don't worry. You don't have to. We are all praying for you. You can pray for the people who are praying for you."

I loved that. And I did not feel alone.

Surrendering Our Own Bodies

Nature doesn't always wait for us to hand over our toys. Sometimes she takes them away without our permission. When I was sixteen, I memorized a poem that struck me even then with its poignant truth about the cycle of life. In his poem "Nature," Henry Wadsworth Longfellow (1807–82) compares Nature to a loving mother getting a sleepy child ready for bed. The child looks back at his toys, reluctant to leave them but knowing he must.

> *So Nature deals with us, and takes away*
> *Our playthings one by one, and by the hand*
> *Leads us to rest so gently, that we go*
> *Scarce knowing if we wish to go or stay.*

Some of our broken playthings are our bodies. Breasts droop, bellies expand, hair falls, wrinkles beget wrinkles. Sexual drive may diminish or disappear. Even the fittest among us eventually lose our athletic edge. Our health may become more fragile. Here, letting go means accepting what we can't change with as much tranquility as we can manage. And appreciating and using what we still have.

To let go is to give up the myth that I am in control. Or that I'll live forever. We may intellectually acknowledge that we will die, but we secretly believe we'll be an exception. When I was a judge, one of my colleagues fell in the court garage and broke his hip. He was indignant. "I never expected anything like this to happen!" He was ninety-three years old.

As we age, some of us gracefully accept our slowing gait or need for bifocals. Others want to look eternally young. Joan Rivers looked thirty when she died at eighty. But it cost her a lot of money, physical discomfort, and, one imagines, anxiety. And she died. She did go out as she wanted, though: "looking good."

I'm more and more aware that I'm not the independent, self-sufficient actor I pretend to be. In fact, I never have been. I will continue to do as much as I can, but increasingly I'll need the help of others. Acceptance of this can be the path to tranquility. Mother Theresa said we lack peace because we've forgotten that we belong to each other. To acknowledge my need of others blesses them and me.

But to accept our reality is not to give up. My friend Rick, barely sixty, is my hero. Nearly blind and getting worse, he reads with a large magnifying glass. He's learning Braille. He has stopped driving at night and probably should stop altogether, but he lives in a sub-urb where public transportation is slow and often unavailable. He plays piano beautifully, but his music has to be digitally enlarged so he can read the notes. Nevertheless, Rick perseveres. He has begun to volunteer his computer skills with organizations that support people with disabilities. He's brave. But sometimes, in the stillness of the night, I imagine he weeps. It's not easy to let go of our bodies.

Old people are not the only ones who are called to relinquish-ment. One day I got into a court elevator with a tall, slim, dark-haired young man I'll call Mike. Somewhere between parking and the second floor, he blurted out, "Judge, I have AIDS." He was thirty-four years old when he died.

I won't sentimentalize Mike's last months. I saw the weight drop off. He became unsteady on his feet. He began to lose sight in one eye. He had little energy, and his mental abilities deteriorated. Sometimes he was moody or unreasonable. Eventually the disease stripped Mike of everything: he was bedridden, blind, confused, unable to care for himself.

What is left when everything else is gone?

Let me suggest that what is left, what is most human, is the capacity for love.

Mike did not wear a mask. He reinforced for me that I am not a human *doing* or a human *having* but a human *being*, capable of giving love and worthy of receiving it. Mike taught me that there is no point in burdening today with regrets about the past or anxieties about the future. We can't do anything about either. The questions become "How can I live most fully today? Who can I help today? What beauty can I see, appreciate, be grateful for, delight in today?"

Mike understood the joy of living in the present moment, of accepting and even rejoicing in the way things are. When he told me he was going blind, I asked, "How do you keep up your spirits?"

He said, "Well, they told me I can have a seeing-eye dog. I can get him as a puppy. I'm really excited about that, because I always wanted a puppy and never had one."

I called him at his home when he became bedridden. To my surprise, he sounded happy. "I'm having a wonderful day. A beautiful person named Joanna came to my room to cut my hair. She has a terrific voice. She sang me gospel songs while she gave me a haircut."

Mike began to tell me about Joanna, about the pain she had suffered in her life. And I realized that he had given Joanna the gift of compassionate listening, even as she was ministering to him. As sick as he was, he was still able to give and receive love.

As his lungs began to fail, it became harder for Mike to speak. But I will never forget him. His letting go was complete. His last "So-wa-ha!" was not a shout but a whispered prayer.

9

Dying and Death

by Sig

Most Americans say they want to die at home surrounded by loved ones. But a survey taken by the Centers for Disease Control in 2005 showed that only about 25 percent succeeded. According to the CDC survey (also cited on page 87), more of us were dying in hospitals; the rest died in nursing homes or long-term-care facilities. But statistics change: In 2013, Forbes contributor Howard Gleckman observed that more people are now dying at home or in hospice, but those who die in hospitals are getting more intensive care.[1]

Why don't we plan ahead? If we do, then why are our plans not carried out as we had hoped? Why don't we stick to our original desire? What accounts for this disparity? Here are some reasons:

1. We don't know what we want or how to prepare for the inevitable.
2. We postpone making plans because we think we're too young, too healthy, in a state of denial, or it's too soon to think about such contingencies.
3. We're reluctant to discuss with others how we wish to die.
4. We are unaware of how to plan for the unexpected, be it a life-threatening illness or accident or our immediate death.

Opting for the "Heroic" Rather than Home

Despite what many Americans voice, most opt for hospitalization because they and their family members are unaware of the

---

1. Howard Gleckman, "More People Are Dying at Home and in Hospice, but They Are also Getting more Intense Hospital Care," *Forbes* online, February 6, 2013.

risks involved with aggressive, expensive treatments in the hospital that may rob them of their quality of life and the opportunity for loved ones to be at their bedside during their final days. Such life-prolonging care accounts for nearly 30 percent of total Medicare spending. The worst thing is that being in the hospital usually doesn't prolong life. It just prolongs dying.

In *Hard Choices for Loving People*, former nursing home and hospice care chaplain Hank Dunn cites several examples of how so-called heroic measures, such as artificial hydration and feeding and intubation, failed to extend either the longevity of a terminally ill patient or the quality of their lives. He notes, "In cases of terminal illness one form of life prolonging care—cardiopulmonary resuscitation—may represent a positive violation of a person's right to die with dignity." Another, artificial feeding, "does not lengthen the life of an end-stage dementia patient and only adds greater burdens."[2]

In less than eighty pages, Dunn addresses the effects of "heroic measures"—among them, artificial hydration, ventilators, and intubation on terminally ill patients. More than two million copies of his book have been distributed worldwide in English, Spanish, Chinese, and Japanese.

Ellen Goodman, cofounder and director of "The Conversation Project," writes about her mother: "We talked about everything except one thing: how she wanted to live at the end of her life. . . . I realized only after her death how much easier it would have all been if I heard her voice in my ear as these decisions had to be made." Ellen noted that she didn't have such a conversation with her mother before she got dementia. As a result, she was faced with myriad decisions she had no way to resolve because they never had "The Conversation." Ellen's easy-to-navigate conversation Starter Kit guides users on the steps toward talking with family about end-of-life issues. Ellen Goodman's Conversation Project is one of numerous resources available to parents and their adult children when they need to make these decisions (see the resource section at the back of this book).

---

2. Hank Dunn, *Hard Choices for Loving People* (Lansdowne, VA: A & A Publishers, 2009).

I recently learned that a dear friend had chosen hospice care over yet another round of debilitating chemotherapy. It was an enormously tough decision for her and her family. She's only sixty-six, and her zest for life has been infectious to all who know her. Thousands of Americans confront this decision every day, ignorant of what certain suggested life-prolonging treatments will mean.

Imagine if you could view short videos that graphically depict what happens when you undergo emergency, life-saving measures that risk robbing you of any quality of life and could result in your remaining in a hospital until you die. These short videos, produced by Advanced Care Planning Decisions,[3] demonstrate what's involved with treatments such as emergency CPR and breathing tubes. The videos have undergone rigorous review by leading experts in medicine, geriatrics, oncology, cardiology, ethics, and decision-making. Clinical studies show that patients who have viewed these videos have overwhelmingly opted out of costly, life-prolonging treatment.

Founded by Drs. Angelo Volandes and Aretha Delight Davis, this nonprofit foundation features highly qualified clinicians dedicated to educating patients about their choices for medical care. One ACP subscriber commented that the videos "help physicians, their patients, and their patients' families address the issues they need to face around end-of-life care, and make more informed decisions." Another reported that the videos "ensure that patients have the information they need to be active in shared decision-making, and to help physicians understand patients' values and preferences so they can arrive at the right decision together."

Avoiding the Topic: A Personal Story from Carolyn

Death is rarely on our mental or conversational agenda. It is the same for dying. We *wish* for our lives to end in a certain way, but we rarely *plan* for it. If we do plan for it, how likely is it that we share our plans for dying (and death) with our children, loved ones, or friends?

---

3. See www.acpdecisions.org (Advanced Care Planning Decisions).

Whenever my dad heard me express sympathy for a friend with cancer, he'd respond, "What's the big deal about cancer? I've had cancer for twenty years, and I do everything I want to. I just ignore it." It seemed harsh but was mostly true. At seventy, his doctors diagnosed prostate cancer that had spread to his bones. There were lesions on his spine, hip, and sternum. Dad's doctor told Mom he'd be in a wheelchair within two years. But he lived to ninety-three, still able to climb stairs until EMTs carried him off on a stretcher five days before he died.

I say Dad's denial of his cancer was "mostly true" because his last two years became very difficult. He took a lot of pain-killing drugs and fell often but miraculously never broke a bone. And he never complained.

I, on the other hand, used to complain to Jerry about Dad's stubbornness. Dad adamantly refused to sit, even temporarily, in a wheelchair. But since he could not stand for long, his activities with us were limited to church, movies, and eating out. Even though DC has wonderful museums, Dad couldn't take them in. He couldn't visit the zoo with his grandchildren, though he would have enjoyed it. Baseball games, which he used to love, were out. So was traveling—mostly.

One time, Jerry and I were going to a conference in Scottsdale, Arizona. Dad had never seen the desert, and I knew he would love it. But Jerry and I had not invited him along, because we couldn't figure out how he could navigate the airport on his frail legs. Finally, I took the plunge. "Dad," I said. "Would you like to see the desert? Here's where we're going." I showed him pictures of the desert and the red rocks of Sedona.

There was a long pause. "Well," he finally said. "I'd love to go. But I'd be in the way. I can't walk very fast."

"That would be hard in the airport," I agreed. "With luggage and all you have to do with security. But if you'd be willing to use a wheelchair, *just to get you on and off the airplane*, we could do it. In fact, it would help us all get through security quicker."

He thought it over for twenty-four hours and agreed. And he had the time of his life!

Since Dad died, I've had a lot of time to think about his refusal to see himself as a cancer victim. His denial, however, had another price. Because he would not admit he was dying, hospice was never an option. Funeral plans were also forbidden turf.

When Dad reached ninety-three, he began to actively die. He couldn't hold down food and had lost at least forty pounds. He must have known the reason. His body was riddled with the prostate cancer he'd lived with, and minimized, for twenty years. He'd signed an advance directive ("no extraordinary measures") and a health-care power of attorney. But he'd made clear that his own death was not a topic of discussion.

And he was still climbing stairs!

Even though he'd sworn he'd never go back to the hospital, one afternoon he told me to call an ambulance. "I just don't feel right." Early the next morning, in the hospital, he suffered a massive heart attack. A doctor met me in the hall. "He doesn't know what happened. We don't want to frighten him. There's nothing we can do. We'll make him comfortable. He might last twenty-four hours."

I was sad but not surprised. Dad had fought the good fight. I went in to hold his hand. He was alert, even cheery. He pretended nothing had happened. "I feel pretty good," he said through his oxygen mask. "I hope the Redskins win tomorrow." *Denial, full strength. He was not going there.*

But a few hours later he asked, "Why aren't they treating me?"

I tried, "Well, Dad, maybe there's nothing they can do."

He was furious. "I'll fire them and get a new doctor!" He even tried to climb out of bed.

When a woman doctor appeared a couple of hours later, I privately asked her to tell Dad the truth. She was kind. She sat beside him and spoke at eye level. She was indirect and used a lot of silence to let him absorb each sentence.

"Mr. Miller, your daughter tells me you're wondering about treatment." Pause. He nodded. "You've suffered a heart attack." Pause. Nod. "It wasn't a little one." Longer pause. "I'm afraid it did a lot of damage. . . . We can't fix it." A really long pause. "And you know you also have cancer . . . that has spread. That's why you can't keep food down." More silence.

Finally, from Dad, "How long?"

"Not weeks." (Her phrasing astonished me, since the other doctor had predicted twenty-four hours.) "Is there anything you need to do?"

Dad looked at me. "No. You'll take care of Mom." She was in a nursing home with advanced Alzheimer's. "You know about the money . . ." Then he described the funeral he wanted.

The doctor emphasized the things Dad could control. He could choose hospice (which she explained), he could control his pain medication, and he could decide whether he wanted to go home or stay where he was.

When she left, Dad said, "She said I have two weeks."

Nobody argued with him. He lived four more days. I'm glad I didn't try to convince him that his cancer was killing him. There are times when denial may be the most compassionate, even realistic path.

Who Should Break the News?

Then there is Gail's story. She was put into an extremely awkward situation when her mother's oncologist said, "Your mom has terminal cancer. You should tell her."

Gail and her mother lived in different cities. And Gail's mother had an appointment with the oncologist only two days later. Gail wondered, *What should I do? Is it ethical for my mother's doctor to leave it up to me to tell her she has an untreatable cancer? Isn't that the doctor's responsibility*? How should one frame a message that is as heart-wrenching as informing your parent that her days are literally numbered?

Once you've taken that step and bravely, and perhaps tearfully, broken the fateful news, how do you respond to such questions as "How serious is the cancer? How long do I have to live? Are there treatments that will possibly cure, or if not cure, then can we delay the inevitable? Will they be able to control the pain?" And worst of all, what should Gail's reply be if her mother asks, "What do you think I should do?"

Chances are that the doctor did not want to tell Gail's mother himself because he didn't know what to say. Dr. Atul Gawande, author of *Being Mortal*, urges medical schools to train doctors how to talk about death and dying. Carolyn's dad's doctor knew how to do it and did it right.

Well, Gail broke the news to her mother. It couldn't have been easy telling her parent that she was going to die . . . soon. Gail also promised to come home to accompany her Mom to her appointment. Gail's mother received the news with equanimity. Knowing that Gail's knowledge was limited and that she had an appointment with the oncologist two days later, her mother had only one request of Gail: that she be strong, because she would need her daughter's fortitude and love more than ever in the months to come.

"Death Cafés"

The ways in which we can talk about death and dying are manifold. One bizarre example is a public comment by Japan's finance minister in 2013 urging older Japanese citizens "to hurry up and die." Concerned about escalating medical costs for Japan's burgeoning senior population, he issued this less than appropriate remark.[4]

A more comfortable (and novel) way to discuss the topic of death is to attend a "death café." Conceived by a Swiss sociologist, the idea has spread to the United Kingdom, France, and more recently to the United States. A "death café," we are assured, provides a respectful and confidential setting for persons to share their thoughts about the kind of death they envision for themselves.

While Carolyn and I were taken aback when we first read the term, we felt the concept was worth examining. For too long, the topic of death has been among the "forbidden fruit" of polite conversation. The idea of a formal setting in which to discuss death (whether it's called a "death café" or something less blunt) brings the subject of death out of the closet.

Death cafés are informal gatherings where participants talk about death and dying from their personal perspective. A hospice worker organized the first one in the United States in Columbus, Ohio, after being encouraged by how willing people were to discuss

---

4. Reported in *The Guardian*, January 22, 2013.

death when she explained her occupation. "People," she said, "feel a need to talk about death."

Think about it: Why not ask a loved one who may be dying what kind of funeral he or she would like to have? I suggest we all try it, if only once. Share with them how you hope to spend your final days. Do we want to die in a hospital or at home or somewhere else? In sum, wouldn't we be better off if we could openly discuss the kind of death we envision for ourselves? It's time we unearthed the tough conversation around death and what we'd like to happen when our "time" rolls around.

To that end, I decided to attend one of these cafés where discussion about death and dying turned out to be frank and open. I met with twelve others (I was the only male). One by one, we talked about how we wish to die and about our experiences with loved ones who had died recently. As we discussed our expectations and experiences, it dawned on me that this was a "permission-giving" process. In other words, as one speaker after another loosened up and shared their thoughts, others felt free to jump in. The conversation ranged from the intimate to the humorous, from the loss of a child to planning our own funerals.

After stressing the need for confidentiality, the facilitator asked us to explain why we decided to attend the café and then to complete this sentence: "Death is _____." Some of the one-word replies were "transition," "painful," "peaceful," and "necessary." She next asked us to reflect on "contradictions in our thoughts about death." Someone suggested that suicide has its contradictions. While a person committing suicide may think they are ending their physical or emotional pain, they rarely consider the pain their death may inflict on their loved ones.

The questions we also discussed—"How do I want to die?" "Where do I want to spend my last days?" "And with whom?"— were similar to those thoughtfully posed by the award-winning PBS documentary, *Consider the Conversation*.[5]

_____

5. *Consider the Conversation: A Documentary on a Taboo Subject*, produced by Burning Hay Wagon Productions (Jefferson, WI: 2011), https://considertheconversation.org/.

Documentary: *Consider the Conversation*

This production is a rare find. Consisting of interviews with hospice workers, doctors, an ALS patient, and numerous others, it challenges us to think about how we both hope and plan to spend our final days. In an accompanying study guide, the producers state that their goals include "changing the commonly held American view that end-of-life is a failed medical event rather than a normal process rich in opportunity for human development." Second, they seek to inspire dialogue between patient and doctor, husband and wife, parent and child, minister and parishioner. Third, they want to encourage medical professionals, health-care workers, and clergy to take the lead in counseling others about end-of-life issues.

The documentary does not offer answers. Instead, it poses questions all of us need to contemplate and answer for ourselves. The film elegantly aligns these questions with the concept of advance care planning, which focuses on talking with patients and loved ones about their end-of-life wishes, documenting them, and taking action to ensure they're honored. The film also ponders: At what point is the quality of life no longer worth the emotional and physical costs of maintaining it? When is it okay to acknowledge that one has fought the good fight, and it's now all right to accept moving to the next phase? Have we had a tough conversation with our doctor about end-of-life planning? Will our doctor be honest and courageous enough to tell us when there is no more they can do? Do they view death not as a medical failure but a fact of life? When is enough enough?

It seems that almost every day there is a new website devoted to this topic. Take, for example, "It's Okay to Die When You Are Prepared" (www.oktodie.com). Created by Dr. Monica Williams-Murphy and Kristian Murphy, its mission—like other sites on death and dying—is to help people understand the importance of planning ahead, making their peace, understanding that it is *okay to die* naturally, and knowing which choices will allow them to pass away peacefully and comfortably, surrounded by those who love them most.

The authors of "Okay to Die" believe that public discussion of issues related to death and dying will have the added benefits of healing personal relationships, strengthening communities, and even politically unifying the nation. Their checklists offer readers six pages of suggestions on preparing for their own death.

If only we could have such free and open-ended conversations with those we love and cherish most. What restrains us from initiating a conversation about death with family, or even with our doctor?

End of Life: The Doctor's Role

Consulting with a medical professional about end-of-life planning seems, at first glance, sensible. Ideally, doctors should have the most expertise in assisting us prepare our end-of-life plans. But how many of us actually consult with our doctors about this? Some of us may hesitate to contact our doctors, because we are unaccustomed to discussing these issues with anyone outside our family circle. Whether you should include your doctor in this process relies on three factors:

1. Will your physician be reimbursed (by Medicare or another government-funded program) to counsel you on end-of-life planning and care?

2. Does your doctor appreciate your need to know your options regarding end-of-life care, treatment, and planning?

3. Does your medical professional have the appropriate training and knowledge to conduct such a conversation?

After 2010, the US Government finally authorized reimbursing physicians who counseled their patients about end-of-life care options, such as advance medical directives, sometimes referred to as living wills, by which a patient requests or foregoes life-sustaining treatment under certain circumstances.

Some doctors may include an explanation of end-of-life planning such as pain management and hospice care in these consultations. In this way doctors can learn how their patients wish to be treated should they become too ill to decide for themselves or voice their preferences. Also, medical professionals are assured they will be reimbursed for their time and hearing firsthand what kind of care their patients desire if and when they can no longer communicate their wishes.

According to research published in the *British Medical Journal*,[6] advance care planning actually improves end-of-life treatment, increases patient and family satisfaction, and reduces stress, anxiety, and depression among surviving relatives. Just as important, end-of-life consultations can also reduce health-care system costs by eliminating unnecessary testing and procedures that patients may not want or need.[7]

The consultation is ideally intended to put the patient in control of how they wish to be treated in case of a terminal illness or a life-threatening accident. This can be a boon for families who have avoided such "tough conversations" in the past.

Palliative Care

Another problem is that doctors don't grasp the importance for patients to understand their options regarding end-of-life planning and care. One option that doctors often fail to mention (or hesitate to suggest) is palliative care.

"We would like to confer with a palliative care doctor" were the words that produced a positive "Moment of Change" for Dina Keller Moss, a health-care analyst in Maryland and former remote caregiver for her late mother who lived in New York City.[8]

Moss felt torn. She and a physician had been discussing radical surgeries with drastic quality-of-life implications for her mother, who suffered from a colorectal mass. Should she follow her hospitalized eighty-nine-year-old mother's longstanding health-care instructions calling for *no* "invasive procedures," *no* chemo or ra-

---

6. "The Impact of Advance Care Planning on End of Life Care in Elderly Patients: Randomised Controlled Trial," *British Medical Journal* (March 24, 2010).

7. From Dr. Sharon Brangman in 2010, then president-elect of the American Geriatrics Society and Chief of Geriatrics, SUNY Upstate Medical University in Syracuse, New York.

8. Dina Keller Moss, "I Almost Blew My Mother's Last Wish," *The Washington Post*, July 18, 2017.

diation, and *no* life-prolonging treatments, or encourage her to undergo a complicated procedure with dubious outcomes?

After Moss checked with her mother's friends and a previous caregiver, she seriously questioned this last option. When she mentioned the possibility of palliative care to the hospital's discharge physician, he said he was trained in the field. What followed was a course of treatment that permitted her mother to die a dignified and mostly pain-free death several months later.

What concerned Moss was that her mother's physician never mentioned palliative care as an option.

> Clearly his rosy picture of life after surgery and his assessment of the alternatives were based on his own values, fears, and preferences rather than those expressed by my mother, an elderly woman who above all else feared a longer and increasingly limited existence. . . . [H]e was either ignoring or ignorant of the potential mitigation of pain and suffering available through effective palliative care.[9]

In 2010, New York State enacted a Palliative Care Information Act requiring that all patients facing an illness or condition to be "fully informed of the options available to them . . . so they are empowered to make choices consistent with their goals for care and wishes and beliefs and to optimize their quality of life."

If you have a terminally ill parent or loved one in an ICU and there is little hope they will live much longer, the patient (maybe with your support) may opt for care that offers comfort and some semblance of a better quality of life, *if* they are made aware of such care. The problem, as noted in a 2014 Institute of Medicine Report, is that "many people nearing the end of life are not physically or cognitively able to make their own care decisions."

"The majority of these patients will receive acute hospital care from physicians who do not know them."[10] Therefore, advance care

---

9. Dina Keller Moss, "Narrative Matters: Getting It Right at the End of Life," *Health Affairs* 36, no. 7 (July 2017): 1336–39; excerpted in *The Washington Post*, July 18, 2017, E-1, E-5.

10. *Dying in America: Improving Quality and Honoring Individual Preferences near the End of Life*, Institute of Medicine Report Brief (September 2014), 12, www.iom.edu/end.

planning is essential to ensure that patients receive care reflecting their values, goals, and preferences. Of people who indicate end-of-life care preferences, most choose care focused on alleviating pain and suffering. However, because the default mode of much hospital treatment is acute care, advance planning and medical orders are needed to ensure that these preferences are honored.

Palliative care (sometimes referred to as "comfort care") is patient-centered as opposed to traditional physician- or institutional-centered models. Its goal is to improve the quality of life and alleviate the pain, stress, and discomfort of patients (and their families) with a serious illness. A team of palliative care specialists—physicians, nurses, and social workers—begin by learning about a patient's priorities, symptoms, and other problems, whether social, emotional, or spiritual, and then work to ensure that the care they provide is aligned and coordinated with the needs of that patient as a whole person.

A "Report Card" published in 2015 by the Center to Advance Palliative Care (CAPC) contains a state-by-state assessment of palliative care programs in our nation's hospitals.[11] Check the "Report Card" to learn how many hospitals in your state provide palliative care and have staff members trained in this field. Some states—such as Ohio, Vermont, and Nevada—received an A. Others—such as Arkansas, Wyoming, and New Mexico—received a D.

While similar in many ways, differences exist between palliative and hospice care.[12] Palliative care is about providing relief from symptoms such as pain, fatigue, constipation, and depression. It is provided to people with a debilitating illness, whether or not they are improving, and for an indefinite period. It can be administered at the same time as a curative treatment.

On the other hand, an ill person entering hospice anticipates no possibility of a cure. Hospice care is provided at the end of someone's life. The care received in hospice is palliative only; curative care is foregone. (Patients can change their mind and seek curative

---

11. "America's Care of Serious Illness," Center to Advance Palliative Care, www.reportcard.capc.org.

12. Trisha Torrey, "The Difference between Hospice and Palliative Care," August 1, 2016, www.verywell.com.

care, but this may terminate their right to hospice for a time.) Hospice care is usually limited to six months and covered by Medicare if the patient is sixty-five years or older, or Medicaid if the patient qualifies financially.

To enter a hospice program (at home or as an in-patient in a nursing or separate hospice institution), a doctor (or in some states, two doctors) must certify that a patient is not expected to live more than six months. Some patients, like Carolyn's dad, do not want to acknowledge this; they can still receive palliative care, but they will lose some services provided by hospice (such as free medical supplies and equipment, visits from a nurse, limited services from a home health aide, access to music therapy, bereavement counseling, and a twenty-four-hour line for a doctor).

Both hospice and ordinary palliative care allow the patient—whether terminally ill or not—to remain at home. Both are appropriate at any age and can be administered at the same time. Both leave decision-making to the patient whether they are terminally or seriously ill. A terminally ill patient who opts for palliative care implicitly agrees to take responsibility for how they wish to spend their remaining days.

Medical professionals (whom we would expect to be best qualified to discuss the matter) often fail or don't know how to counsel their patients on end-of-life matters. Dr. Atul Gawande, a public health researcher and author of *Being Mortal*,[13] wrote in a *New York Times* op-ed piece titled "The Best Possible Day":

> In medicine and society, we [the medical profession] have failed to recognize that people have priorities that they need us to serve besides just living longer. . . . [T]he best way to learn those priorities is to ask about them. Hence the wide expert agreement that payment systems [such as Medicare] should enable health professionals to take sufficient time to have such discussions and tune care accordingly.

Gawande also contends that many doctors lack the knowledge or skill to carry out such conversations:

---

13. Atul Gawande, *Being Mortal: Medicine and What Matters Most* (New York: Henry Holt, 2014).

Medicine has forgotten how vital such matters are to people as they approach life's end. People want to share memories, pass on wisdom and keepsakes, connect with loved ones, and to make some lasting contributions to the world. These moments are among life's most important, for both the dying and those left behind. And the way we in medicine deny people these moments, out of obtuseness and neglect, should be cause for our unending shame.[14]

Our Role: Beth, Rebecca, and Sheila

This puts the responsibility where it rightfully belongs: on us. So, what should we do? More to the point, what *do* we do?

Experiences differ. In our mediation work and in countless conversations with friends and professionals in the field of geriatric care and medicine, we learn from others' experiences. Their stories have become our teaching medium. (In the following stories, we have changed the names and, in some circumstances, the places where they take place. It's the essence that matters.)

Beth

Beth's cancer had metastasized through most of her body. After taking part in several clinical trials, she and her husband concluded that it wasn't worth going through yet another. Her daughter disagreed: "Mom, you have to keep trying. Don't give up." But Beth reluctantly concluded that "it was over." She and the good folks from hospice arranged for her to spend her final weeks at home receiving sufficient palliative care to relieve her pain but allowing her to spend quality time with family and friends.

Her grandchildren drew pictures about Beth and strung them across her front yard. Her sister and her (now reconciled) daughter arranged a visitors' roster, so she would not be overwhelmed but still be able to share time with them through most of the day. When her end was near, the mood was somber, but family and friends continued to visit Beth.

---

14. Atul Gawande, "The Best Possible Day," *New York Times*, October 5, 2014, https://www.nytimes.com/2014/10/05/opinion/sunday/the-best-possible-day .html.

Something else happened: the mourning process began not at Beth's death but while she was dying. In time, she drifted away from all of us. A quiet acceptance permeated her home. Her time had come. And the memorial service held a few weeks later turned out to be a celebration of her amazing accomplishments, as well as her profound humanity.

Rebecca

It was the same with another friend, Rebecca. After several years of relentless chemo and radiation to check her cancer, Rebecca decided to die with dignity. She consulted with family members and some close friends and then contacted a nearby hospice.

Whatever "tough conversations" there might have been were brief, open, and honest. How could anyone object to Rebecca's decision after all the various treatments she had undergone? Everyone was in the loop: family members, close friends, some neighbors, and a few former colleagues. When Rebecca became so weak that she could no longer eat or take care of herself, we all knew it was time.

I recall that one of Rebecca's last cognitive acts was to view a DVD of her grandson performing in a piano recital. Then she rested, grateful for having seen his artistic triumph. For the three or four weeks that she lay in bed, a constant stream of family, friends, and neighbors visited her. She lay in her furnished basement apartment. Soft music penetrated the space. A scented candle burned. Each visitor brought his or her own special treatment "modality." Some sang, others massaged her limbs, and a few talked quietly, reminiscing about happier times they had spent together. What was so impressive was the solace that pervaded the room.

Except for the early hours of each day, Rebecca was never alone. When she died, everyone was at peace . . . with her and with ourselves. We felt sad but not depressed. I learned that her last breaths were labored and short. Then nothing. We all shared a part in Rebecca's passing. Because she gave us a bond we will never forget, our gratitude to her is boundless. She allowed us to be part of her vigil of peace.

Sheila

A year or so after Sheila completed the one-hundred-forty-mile trek along the Camino Trail in northern Spain, she contracted lung cancer. We would say Sheila was a "health nut." She watched every morsel of food she consumed, was in robust health, and exercised daily.

Sheila opted not to try customary cancer treatments. She preferred to live out her remaining months with her daughter and granddaughter as pain free as possible with help from hospice. Just days before her death, her daughter arranged for family members and close friends to celebrate Sheila's seventieth birthday with her. During the party, we each were permitted five minutes of "private time" with her. Those moments will remain with each of us for the rest of our lives.

These are stories of "good deaths." Of people who prepared in advance for their passing and who made tough decisions after having "tough conversations" with family, friends, and perhaps their physicians. Imagine how each will be remembered. This is, indeed, a good legacy as well.

Death with Dignity

More and more Americans are looking for opportunities to exert some measure of control over where and how they die. Nearly fifteen years ago, Bill Moyers produced and narrated a documentary titled *A Death of One's Own*. In it, he depicts the deaths of three persons suffering from terminal illness. With compassion and patience, he unravels the complexities underlying the many choices at the end of life, including the bitter debate over physician-assisted suicide. These patients, their families, and their doctors discuss some of the hardest decisions, including how to pay for care, what constitutes humane treatment, and how to balance dying and dignity. In the end, did these patients die the way they wanted? Yes . . . and no.

As of this writing (August 2018), multiple states—Oregon, New Mexico, Vermont, California, Colorado, Hawaii, Washington, and the District of Columbia—have enacted laws allowing one form or another of physician-assisted suicide. (Hawaii's statute, passed in 2018, becomes effective January 1, 2019. Montana has no statute, but the state Supreme Court declared that it is not a crime under the state constitution for a doctor to give medical assistance in dying.)[15] It's important to note that in most of these states the law is under attack.[16]

The leading proponent of physician-assisted suicide is the Death with Dignity National Center. Its website (www.deathwith dignity.org) offers a wealth of information for those interested in the issue. The center was formed out of a commitment to the idea that personal end-of-life decisions should be made solely between a patient and a physician.

Compassion and Choices (www.compassionandchoices.org) is another resource that addresses death with dignity and patient-centered end-of-life care. In addition to educating individuals about making informed decisions about care, it also describes how one can request from one's doctor medications to self-administer to help death be as peaceful as possible. Its professional staff, "end-of-life volunteers," and trained counselors work with thousands of clients each year, explaining options and offering nonjudgmental support to help them make and communicate their decisions. Its "Good to Go Resource Guide" tells readers how to prepare an ad-vance directive and details how anyone can be assured their wishes will be met when facing a life-ending illness.

The question of suicide to end one's suffering is not a simple one. Aside from religious strictures, let's not forget how others can be impacted by these situations—namely, the caregivers, especially spouses, adult children, or other loved ones.

Joe, the youngest of a large family and his mother's caregiver, knew how much pain she endured with her abdominal cancer. "I want to die . . . now," she told him, over and over. One day when his sister was visiting, Mom started moaning. Against Mom's wishes, the sister called an ambulance. Mom refused to go, and Joe de-

---

15. *Baxter v. Montana*, 224 P3d 1211 (2009).
16. See https://www.deathwithdignity.org/learn/death-with-dignity-acts/.

fended her decision. The ambulance drove away, empty. Joe's sister stormed out, hurt and furious.

The next week Joe's mother called each of her children. She said, "I probably won't see you again. I want you to know I love you." When she had completed all her calls, she took her own life.

While Joe didn't know what she planned to do and he played no role in it, he was not surprised. But his siblings said, "You could have stopped her." They not only blamed him, but they also shunned him. Now Joe says, "I have no family."

This is where the legacy question enters. In a compelling blog recently posted by A Place for Mom, a national senior living referral service, we are reminded that preparing for the loss of a loved one is critical for caregivers. Too often, we prepare more for a vacation than for loss and death, contends Shelly Whizin, a certified death midwife.[17]

Four Things to Say

There are things we can do during this time of dying that may give you and the person you love better peace of mind—such as saying to someone who is dying these four short sentences:

1. Please forgive me.

2. I forgive you.

3. Thank you.

4. I love you.

In his book *The Four Things That Matter Most*, hospice and palliative care specialist Dr. Ira Byock writes that these are the words dying people long to hear and say. We might be able to say them to a dying person we love. As Dr. Byock says, however, they can also change our relationships with the living. But this isn't always easy.[18]

---

17. See www.sswhizin.com.
18. Ira Byock, *The Four Things That Matter Most: A Book about Living* (New York: Free Press, 2004).

Why? Because we are afraid to appear weak or even vulnerable. Vulnerability can be tough. Do we feel we're putting ourselves in a "one down" or "one up" relationship? For instance, a parent may have trouble apologizing to a child. Or a boss to an employee. Will admitting we are wrong diminish us in the other's eyes? Will we lose face? Are we afraid to be hurt or rejected if we reveal our feelings? What if I apologize and the other person refuses to forgive me? What if I express love and the other person remains silent? What if I thank someone, and they say, "It's about time!" What if I tell someone I forgive them and they say, "I didn't do anything wrong. You're too sensitive."

Remember the legacy: At least we've made the stretch and tried to put things right.

We don't have to wait for old age or approaching death to do this. Carolyn's wise and compassionate friend Patty Wedel runs Joseph's House, a hospice for formerly homeless men and women with AIDS and other terminal illnesses. Many of her guests have a history of drug addiction, mental illness, or prison. Relating to them is not always easy.

I want to share some words from Patty's Christmas letter about meeting others where they are:

> At Joseph's House we sometimes say to each other, "Don't wait!" When we say this we mean *Don't wait for a situation or a person to be otherwise in order to bring ourselves fully to it or to them with loving kindness.*

> This reminder helps so much! In an ordinary, everyday way it helps us gradually to learn to love as is, with no conditions. We bring our whole self to this person, this situation—just as it is, as we are—and it's enough. It's good.

Whatever Our Age: We Can Have Conversations That Bless

In a wonderful book, *My Grandfather's Blessings*, Dr. Rachel Naomi Remen tells of childhood conversations she had with her grandfather, an Orthodox Jewish rabbi.[19] Every afternoon when she came home from school, they shared tea and he told her stories. His stories guided Naomi's entire life.

When she was four years old, he told her a story of creation. A great ball of darkness broke up into countless sparks of light that were scattered throughout the universe. There is a God-spark in everyone and everything. To listen and to notice the light in others is to heal the world. He told her that we are born to bless and serve life. He himself had a blessing for everything, and he taught many of them to Naomi.

When Naomi was seven, she and her grandfather had a very difficult conversation. He was sick, and he told her he was dying. He said he would be going somewhere else, closer to God. He said she wouldn't be able to visit him there, "but I will watch over you and I will bless those who bless you."

Now in her seventies, Dr. Remen says her life has been blessed by a great many people, and each of them has been her grandfather's blessing. She has passed it on. After years as a pediatrician, she began to lead support groups for doctors who were treating cancer patients and carrying enormous grief they couldn't express. Then she expanded to treat cancer patients themselves and others suffering from incurable diseases.

Herself a victim of Crohn's disease since age fifteen, she now helps people find meaning in their own suffering—and she teaches them to bless life, to bless others. These blessings are spread through conversations, some of them tough: stories, listening, sharing compassion.

Dr. Remen says, "The power of our blessing is not diminished by illness or age." It's something we can do until we die. We can choose to live so that our struggles and memories will give hope to others when they remember us after we are gone. That is a good legacy.

---

19. Rachel Naomi Remen, *My Grandfather's Blessings* (New York: Riverhead Books, 2000).

10

Toward a Shared World

by Sig

Words such as *family* and *community* usually connote some level of understanding, positive interaction, and consensus. Or maybe not. A "family" can live in a state of strife and be engulfed in misunderstanding.

The word *community* might suggest commonality of interests, goals, and procedures. Or a group of people incapable of bridging their differences. Building community can be challenging, or even impossible. The same goes for a family.

Shift gears for a moment. What happens when friends sit down for a Thanksgiving dinner in America, or two families are joined in a wedding ceremony in India, or Olympic athletes parade into a sports stadium anywhere? A flash mob begins singing in a railroad terminal and engages the attention of passersby? For a moment, or an hour or longer, people from different backgrounds, traditions, and points of view share a unifying activity. Be it a victory celebration, attending a funeral, or sitting at the bedside of a dying family member, a shared world emerges.

As mediators, we experience shared worlds after adversaries reach a mutually acceptable settlement and then—together—devise ways to carry it out. Enemies become allies, if only to fulfill their agreement. Political rivals unite to approve a single measure they both support. Afterward, they'll likely return to their previous relationship.

What then is a "shared world"? A shared world develops when people find themselves engaged in the same effort and agree on how to address it. It's the moment when they understand that their pasts should not interfere with whatever common goal they've set out to

achieve. It's a time when family members can set aside their differences and agree on caregiving for a terminally ill parent. When
this happens, two forces are at work. One brings people together
and keeps the group intact. Another is their preparedness to work
in concert for a common goal.

A shared world does not depend on both parties—or family
members—fully understanding each other or agreeing with other.
A shared world may emerge when housed people understand the
cruelty of homelessness, when a volunteer in a soup kitchen sees
hunger up close, when the mentor of a foster child grasps how
poverty can thwart personal achievement.

Now think of your family: you and your parents, or your adult
children, may not have inhabited a truly shared world for many
years. Family members may reside in different cities or coun-
tries, pursue separate lives, and hold on to entrenched conflicts
stemming from childhood. Tensions still bubble up, and grudges
remain entrenched. The previous pages have addressed ways
to diminish these tensions, dissolve grudges, and renew, even
strengthen, relationships. You may have overcome some of these
difficulties, or not. At least, you now know that tools exist to repair
torn relationships.

Something happens when adult children understand how de-
meaning it is for parents when they can no longer undertake what
they easily carried out ten or fifteen years earlier. When they see
parents move from their home of forty years into an independent
or assisted living residence. Or grasp their feelings of helplessness
when they can no longer drive, prepare meals, or handle their finances. Or experience the indignities of aging when they fail to
navigate the Internet or find the supermarket or remember a grandchild's birthday. A shared world emerges when parents appreciate
that their children ask to help with caregiving and want to know
about their health, well-being, and end-of-life plans.

A shared world comes about when siblings agree on common
action to support an aging parent, instead of taking sides against
one another. If only for a year or two while Mom is in skilled nursing or Dad is in hospice, if they can set aside unresolved differences
and unhealed wounds, then they can convene *their* shared world.

Here's what a shared world might look like: Adult children are informed about their parents' health, medications, and doctors. They know how to handle a medical emergency. They have *in their possession* copies of their parents' health-care and general powers of attorney and the names and contact information of their doctors, accountant, and attorney. They know and respect their parents' preferences for Mom's or Dad's funeral or memorial service and what financial arrangements exist after the parent dies—where the original copy of the will resides and even the disposition of their parents' assets—and their hopes for their children.

A shared world becomes apparent when parents feel confident that their children understand their caregiving concerns and their need to retain some semblance of independence as their capacity to live alone recedes; that children will honor their financial plans and help with housekeeping responsibilities; and that their adult children can willingly assume these responsibilities and not gripe about who does what.

In other words, everyone is in the know. Transparency reigns. Trust triumphs. A shared world is not the pinnacle of perfection, nor does it hold the promise of perfect peace. It doesn't mean that all intra-family grievances are erased or that long-held jealousies evaporate. The Olympic athletes celebrating the opening of the games know that the next day they will be competing against one another.

You and your family members may not experience the exhilaration of athletes taking part in an Olympic opening ceremony, or what musicians must feel after performing a Brahms symphony, or a sailing crew after winning the America's Cup. Still, for however long it takes, a team approach always takes precedence over freelancing and collaboration takes priority over individual preference.

Now take stock of your family: How close is it to becoming a shared world? What steps are needed to bring about the kind of world you'd like to inhabit as your parents age and as you understand and support their goals?

Afterword

by Carolyn and Sig

When we set out to write this book, we had one goal in mind: To show families how to live in peace as parents age. We have seen, touched, and felt the suffering that family members can endure because they are afraid to speak with one another about things that matter most. We wanted to help.

We have also seen and touched the joy and relief children and parents feel when they have listened deeply to one another and know they have been heard. When family members commit to set aside ancient grievances and the need to "win," they discover a vast field beyond each person's ideas of wrong and right answers. Despair recedes. Multiple solutions for issues emerge into view. As the poet Rumi says, "When the soul lies down in that grass / the world is too full to talk about."

Paradoxically, talking about it is what takes us to that field. We want to share and make explicit some ethical principles that have guided our work with families, and which we think families themselves should consider when conflicts arise.

First, elders should participate in any discussions about them, whenever possible. Our elder mediation training in 2013 stressed this, and our experience confirms it. No end-runs by the kids. No behind-closed-doors discussions about taking away car keys. No conspiratorial plans about nursing homes or throwing out the "junk" Mom has been collecting for thirty years.

Second, if—despite everyone's mutual efforts and goodwill—the family still can't agree, then the parents should win. Their decisions about their own money, health, friends, and living arrangements should prevail, simply because every competent adult deserves the dignity of having their autonomy respected.

Third, ethical obligations run both ways. Elders, what kind of legacy will you leave behind? Parents who hope to be lovingly remembered must recognize with compassion the stresses on sandwich-generation grown-ups with careers, bills, and children of their own. Parents should also acknowledge their children's needs for family transparency, for reassurance of the parent's love, for the comfort of knowing the status of a parent's health, and the content of a parent's well-made plans.

We know this isn't easy, but you can do it! As a family, you will emerge stronger, braver, more loving, making new memories together—and closer than ever before.

RESOURCE GUIDE

The resources listed below have in some way informed our understanding of the problems and challenges facing families as they confront the multiple but intertwined worlds of aging, conversation, sibling issues, legal and medical concerns, caregiving, dying, and death. A full list of print and digital resources would likely equal the length of this book and be outdated before the print has dried, but we think we've provided enough to get you started!

Chapter 1. Not Your Grandma's Old

Applewhite, Ashton. *This Chair Rocks: A Manifesto against Ageism.* New York: Networked Books, 2016.

The author traces her journey from apprehensive boomer to pro-aging radical, and in the process explains the roots of ageism and our own age denial and how it divides and debases us.

Friedman, Marc. *The Big Shift: Navigating the New Stage beyond Midlife.* New York: PublicAffairs, 2012.

Friedman charts a new migration across time as millions transition from middle age to a new encore phase that is characterized by purpose, contribution, and commitment, particularly to the well-being of future generations.

Goldsmith, Theodore C. *Aging by Design: How New Thinking on Aging Will Change Your Life.* Rev. ed. Azinet Press, 2011.

For anyone interested in theories of aging, author Goldsmith presents a well-rounded and carefully documented and referenced guide.

Greenbaum, Stuart, ed. *Longevity Rules: How to Age Well into the Future*. Carmichael, CA: Eskaton Senior Residences and Services, 2010.

An excellent collection of short essays spanning the political, economic, medical, societal, and behavioral aspects of aging.

Gulette, Margaret Morganroth. *Ending Ageism, Or How Not to Shoot Old People*. New Brunswick, NJ: Rutgers University Press, 2017.

This award-winning author raises urgent legal, economic, and ethical issues to show why anti-ageism should be the next social movement of our time.

Lindland, E., M. Fond, A. Haydon, and N. Kendall-Taylor. "Gauging Aging: Mapping the Gaps between Expert and Public Understanding of Aging in America." *A Frameworks Strategic Report*. Frameworks Institute, Washington, DC. New York: Simon & Schuster, 2015.

Sarafan, Lily, Kathy N. Johnson, and James H. Johnson. *Happy to 102: The Best Kept Secrets to a Long and Happy Life*. Palo Alto, CA: Home Care Press, 2009.

A short, practical handbook on how centenarians can still lead a rewarding and meaningful existence.

Schacter-Shalomi, Zalman, and Ronald S. Miller. *From Age-ing to Sage-ing: A Revolutionary Approach to Growing Older*. New York: Grand Central, 2014.

The authors show how we can turn "age-ing" into "sage-ing," an adventure that brings more passion, mystery, and meaning into our lives.

Seal, Joan. *Naked at Our Age: Talking Out Loud About Senior Sex*. Berkeley, CA: Seal Press, 2011.

A candid, straight-talking book addressing senior sexuality in all its colors, the challenges, disappointments, and surprises, as well as the delights and the love stories. No topic related to senior sexuality is off limits.

Solie, David. *How to Say It to Seniors: Closing the Communications Gap with Our Elders.* New York: Prentice Hall, 2004.

The author guides us through a maze of developmental roadblocks in order to communicate effectively and compassionately with our elders.

Thomas, Bill. *Second Wind: Navigating the Passage to a Slower, Deeper, and More Connected Life.* New York: Simon & Schuster, 2014.

One of the most innovative thinkers in the field of aging guides us as many of us enter our second coming of age and teaches us to navigate what he contends is the most exciting and challenging developmental stage of life.

Vaillant, George C. *Aging Well: Surprising Guideposts to a Happier Life from the Landmark Harvard Study of Adult Development.* New York: Little Brown, 2002.

Dr. Vaillant draws on the results of a five-decade-long study of the basic elements of adult human development and reveals how some people turn out to be more resilient than others.

Chapter 3. Can We Just Talk?

Bertschler, John, and Patricia Bertschler. *Elder Mediation: A New Solution to Age-Old Problems.* Seven Hills, OH: National Conflict Solutions, 2009.

The authors guide any aspiring elder mediation practitioners on how to set up and market an elder mediation practice.

Chast, Roz. *Can't We Talk about Something More Pleasant? A Memoir.* New York: Bloomsbury, 2014.

Combining humor and pathos, the New Yorker Magazine *cartoonist chronicles the time when she was caregiver to her aging parents.*

The Conversation Project. http://www.theconversationsproject.org.

A practical, multilingual guide for family members in search of ways to discuss end-of-life wishes for themselves and their loved ones.

Smith, Shauna L., *Making Peace with Your Adult Children: A Guide to Family Healing*. New York: Harper Perennial, 1993.

An invaluable guide to healing family rifts and ending the cycle of pain in present and future generations.

Chapter 5. Siblings in War and Peace

Kardasis, Arline, Rikk Larsen, Crystal Thorpe, and Blair Trippe. *Mom Always Liked You Best: A Guide for Resolving Family Feuds, Inheritance Battles & Eldercare Crises*. Norwood, MA: Eldercare/Agreement Resources, 2011.

Four veteran elder mediators apply mediation principles and best practices to help us overcome sibling rivalry and successfully address elder care.

Russo, Francine. *They're Your Parents, Too: How Siblings Can Survive Their Parents' Aging without Driving Each Other Crazy*. New York: Bantam Books, 2010.

Ms. Russo guides us from the "old" family to the "new," in which adult children have to come to terms with their aging parents and with their own relationships.

Chapter 6. Scaling the Twin Peaks of Paperwork and Planning

Esperti, Robert A., and Renno L. Peterson. *Loving Trust: The Smart, Flexible Alternative to Wills and Probate*. Rev. ed. New York: Penguin Books, 1991.

The authors offer families a persuasive case for using a trust rather than a will to transfer wealth to the next generation, as well as provide for your parents' well-being as they encounter infirmities.

Five Wishes. http://www.agingwithdignity.org.

Five Wishes has become America's most popular living will program, because it is written in everyday language and helps start and structure important conversations about care in times of serious illness.

I'm Dead, Now What? Important Information about My Belongings, Business Affairs, and Wishes. White Plains, NY: Peter Pauper Press, 2015.

This no-nonsense hardcover spiral planner with the quirky title guides you as you gather those vital details about your contacts, legal matters, health, financial affairs, instructions, and more.

National Health-Care Decisions Day. http://www.nhdd.org.

Each year, April 16 is devoted to encouraging persons of all ages to prepare their advance health care directive. Established by Dr. Nathan Kottamp, NHHD is one of The Conversation Project's efforts to have everyone's wishes for end-of-life care expressed and respected.

Chapter 7. Caring: Giving and Receiving

Gleckman, Howard. *Caring for Your Parents: Inspiring Stories of Families Seeking New Solutions to America's Most Urgent Health Care Crisis.* New York: St. Martin's Press, 2009.

Journalist/scholar Gleckman recounts his (and others') experiences as he confronts the sudden death of one parent and the caregiving needs of another. From there, he surveys caregiving in America and how to overcome its vexing challenges.

Lebow, Grace, and Barbara Kane with Irwin Lebow. *Coping with Your Difficult Older Parents: A Guide for Stressed-Out Children.* New York: Quill, 1999.

This guide presents real-life situations and workable solutions for dealing with difficult elders to which every adult child and professional caregiver can relate.

Marcell, Jacqueline. *Elder Rage or Take My Father . . . Please: How to Survive Caring for Aging Parents.* 2nd ed. Irvine, CA: Impressive Press, 2001.

A detailed and forthright account of the nightmarish effects of dementia told in such a way that readers feel right there with the author, sharing her experience of coping with her father.

Poo, Ai-Gen, with Ariane Conrad. *The Age of Dignity: Preparing for the Elder Boom in a Changing America.* New York: The New Press, 2015.

The author maps out an integrated set of solutions that may strengthen the fraying safety net and give dignity to the thousands of women and immigrants in the caregiving workforce.

Rosofsky, Ira. *Nasty, Brutish and Long: Adventures in Eldercare.* New York: Penguin Books, 2010.

A wake-up call for those who will eventually realize that there are many tragicomic events that may affect them as caregivers or patients. A go-to source on eldercare, especially as it relates to nursing homes.

Sheehy, Gail. *Passages in Care-giving: Turning Chaos into Confidence.* New York: HarperCollins, 2010.

The author of the 1975 New York Times best-seller for three years outlines nine critical steps for effective caregiving—turning chaos into confidence during the most crucial of life stages as she chronicles how she cared for her husband while he battled cancer for ten years.

Viorst, Judith. *Necessary Losses: The Loves, Illusions, Dependencies, and Impossible Expectations That All of Us Have to Give Up in Order to Grow Older.* New York: The Free Press, 1986.

An enormously readable, well-organized journey that gently nudges us from one state to the next, sharing both the author's joys and sorrows.

Weisfeld, Victoria, and Tracy A. Lustig. *The Future of Home Health Care—Workshop Summary.* Forum on Aging, Disability and Independence. National Institute of Medicine and National Research Council. Washington, DC: National Academies Press, 2015. https://www.nap.edu/catalog/21662/the-future-of-home-health-care-workshop-summary.

Chapter 8. Letting Go: The Path to Freedom

Byock, Ira. *The Best Care Possible: A Physician's Quest to Transform Care through the End of Life.* New York: Avery, 2013.

> *Dr. Byock makes a convincing case for alternatives to heroic medical choices and explains the application of palliative care when other options have either failed or threaten a terminally ill person's quality of life.*

Dunn, Hank. *Hard Choices for Loving People: CPR, Artificial Feeding Comfort Care and the Patient with a Life Threatening Illness.* 5th ed. Lansdowne, VA: A & A Publishers, 2009.

> *This handy primer acquaints us with the risks involved for families when considering life-prolonging medical procedures for their aging loved ones suffering from acute and life-threatening illness.*

Chapter 9. Dying and Death

Brody, Jane E. "When a Spouse Dies, Resilience Can Be Uneven." *New York Times*, September 26, 2016.

Dying in America: Improving Quality and Honoring Individual Preferences near the End of Life. Institute of Medicine of the National Academies, 2014.

> *A consensus report from the Institute of Medicine (IOM) found that improving the quality and availability of medical and social services for patients and their families could not only enhance quality of life through the end of life but may also contribute to a more sustainable care system.*

Gawande, Atul. *Being Mortal: Medicine and What Matters in the End.* New York: Henry Holt, 2014.

> *Beautifully written, easy-to-read look at death and dying through the lens of a doctor who watched his physician-father struggle with the system that wanted to keep him alive, regardless of his*

own wishes. Gawande urges medical schools to teach doctors and nurses how to speak and listen to terminally ill patients with compassion and honesty, to allow them to live their last days as they most deeply wish.

Kalanithi, Paul. *When Breath Becomes Air.* New York: Random House, 2016.

A brilliant, thirty-six-year-old neurosurgeon chronicles his own early dying from Stage IV lung cancer and the relationship between doctor and patient, who becomes both.

Morham, Dan. *The Better End, Surviving (and Dying) on Your Own Terms in Today's Medical World.* Baltimore, MD: Johns Hopkins University Press, 2012.

Through compelling real-life stories, Dr. Morham informs readers how they can negotiate the legal and medical maze of end-of-life care for themselves and their loved ones.

Moss, Dina Keller. "Narrative Matters: Getting It Right at the End of Life." *Health Affairs* 36, no. 7 (July 2017).

Volandes, Angelo. *The Conversation: A Revolutionary Plan for End-of-Life Care.* New York: Bloomsbury, 2015. See also www.acpdecisions.org (Advance Care Planning Decisions).

Dr. Volandes describes how we can transcend the "dark side" of end-of-life care—that is being tethered to machines and tubes—and have the good ending most of us prefer: at home, in comfort, and surrounded by loved ones.

About the Authors

Carolyn Miller Parr

This daughter, wife, and mother has also been a judge, pastor, mediator, workshop leader, and family caregiver. She co-authored her late husband Jerry Parr's memoir, *In the Secret Service* (2013), and has been published in *USA Today*, *Redbud Post*, *Ready Magazine*, and *Englewood Review*. She lives on Spa Creek in Annapolis with her husband, James Le Gette.

Sig Cohen

A former US Foreign Service officer with tours in South Asia, Germany, and the UK, Sig is the father of two and grandfather of three. His background includes mediation, writing, fund-raising, and extensive community service. Among his achievements is founding a thriving Jewish community in the Capitol Hill section of Washington, DC.

Carolyn and Sig blog at www.toughconversations.net.